DANGEROUS
GOD

DANGEROUS
GOD

WRATH, VENGEANCE, RECOMPENSE, AND TERROR

Jim Albright

As you cannot judge a book by its cover, so in this case you cannot judge a book by its title. *Dangerous God* is actually a book of good news—terrifyingly good news—because it is a book full of truth about God. Admittedly, it is truth about God that is often overlooked, ignored, or even denied, but it is truth, nonetheless. It is also hard truth in the sense that instead of giving us "warm fuzzies," it causes cold shivers. But it is good truth in that it corrects the lopsided view of God that is common in contemporary Christianity. If you want to know God more as He reveals Himself in the Bible than as we think we want Him to be, you'll be grateful for this book.

DONALD S. WHITNEY: Professor of Biblical Spirituality and Associate Dean, The Southern Baptist Theological Seminary, Louisville, Kentucky; USA

Jim Albright balances our typically skewed view of God by showing us that he is not only merciful, but also wrathful. Euphemistic thinking about God is not truthful thinking about God. God, in fact, is more merciful than we have ever thought because His just judgment is more severe than we have ever thought. This book, as shocking as it might be, is a needed corrective.

JIM ELLIFF: President of Christian Communicators Worldwide and a founding pastor of Christ Fellowship of Kansas City, Missouri, USA

Jim Albright's latest book is an excellent summary of the often-forgotten doctrines of God's wrath and judgment. He calls believers to a serious reconsideration of our weak contemporary ideas of God as merely loving. This book provides a sobering call to the biblical reality of the wrath of God and an honest reminder of the consequences of ignoring the God who judges all.

JIM EHRHARD: Ph.D. of Theology, Professor at Kiev Theological Seminary, Kiev, Ukraine

Christianity in America has become very man-centered, resulting in the avoidance and neglect of God's wrath, vengeance, recompense, and terror. When I think deeply about a being who will condemn human souls to an eternity of torment but also gladly sacrificed His only Son to a gruesome death to save human souls in rebellion against Him, I'm left in wonderment. Albright focuses on the attributes of God we naturally avoid but so desperately need if we are truly seeking the one, true, living God. As I read *Dangerous God*, the Lord's Spirit deflated my pride, exposed my man-centeredness, and rekindled my fear of the Lord to the praise of His glory and the joy of my soul.

BRAD VADEN: Pastor of Grace Baptist Church, Scott, Arkansas, USA

Albright's new book, *Dangerous God*, is not like any other book you will likely find in the twenty-first century. Albright dares to declare the true nature of the God who inhabits the universe. Many pastors and authors in our fearful-of-offending-others culture shy away from speaking about the true God of the Bible—a God of wrath, anger, and vengeance against sin and sinners...but Jim's book doesn't contain a single "shy" word in it. Jim's not interested in presenting a huggable God that the modern church can easily relate to, but the majestic God that is, the God in whose presence man should tremble. And he's convinced that getting to know this God, and not the domesticated God you've most likely been presented, is the best thing that can happen to you. To live a life in the fear and awe of the living God is truly to live a life worth living. KEITH JONES: Missionary and Founding Pastor of Centro Veritas Church, Milan, Italy

We are quick to use the word "saved" when we refer to people coming to faith in Jesus. We often say, "We are saved from our sins." To somehow believe that we have been saved from something to do with us is a grave error. When through faith in Christ we are saved, we are saved from the wrath of Almighty God. Jim's book shows just what we are saved from and, on the flipside, what we are facing if we do not accept Jesus. This is a no-holds-barred exposé of the God no one wants to talk about because we have applied a "political correctness" filter to our twenty-first-century god that makes Him easier to accept. This book is written in love. It is one of the most honest books about the One True God. You owe it to yourself, your loved ones, and your neighbors to read it. ALAN JOHNSTON: Ordained Minister in the Presbyterian Church of Ireland since 1998; Pastor of Killinchy Presbyterian Church

ISBN : 978-1-7343452-7-8

www.dangerousgod.com

Cover design and typeset by www.greatwriting.org
Cover design consultation: Jim Albright / Olasubomi Onadipe

Great Writing Publications
Taylors, SC
www.greatwriting.org

TABLE OF CONTENTS

". . .It is a terrifying thing to fall into the hands of the living God."

UNPACKING THE TITLE

Dangerous God
Wrath, Vengeance, Recompense, and Terror

Dangerous *adj.* 1. Involving or fraught with danger; perilous. 2. Able or apt to do harm.

God *n.* 1. A being conceived as the perfect, omnipotent, omniscient originator and ruler of the universe, the principal object of faith and worship in monotheistic religions.

Wrath *n.* 1. Violent . . . anger; rage; fury. 2. b. Divine retribution for sin.

Vengeance *n.* 1. The act or motive of punishing another in payment for a wrong or injury he has committed; retribution. 2. With great violence or fury.

Recompense *n.* 2. To . . . make return for. Amends made for something, as damage or loss. Payment in return for something given or done. . . .

Terror *n.* 1. Intense, overpowering fear. 2. Something, as a terrifying object or occurrence, that instills intense fear. 3. The ability to instill intense fear.[2]

The perilous and *apt to do harm* . . . *being conceived as the perfect, omnipotent, omniscient originator and ruler of the universe* . . . has promised *violent anger* and *rage* as *divine retribution for sin.* He will *punish* . . . *with great violence* and *fury* . . . *making payment in return for* . . . what man has *done* . . . resulting *in intense, overpowering, terrifying fear.*

"*God has not only told us the best, but He has not withheld the worst. He has faithfully described the ruin which the Fall has effected. He has faithfully diagnosed the terrible state which sin has produced. He has faithfully made known His enduring hatred of evil, and that He must punish the same. He has faithfully warned us that He is a "consuming fire." [And] His Word . . . records numerous examples of His faithfulness in making good His threatenings.*"[3]

A.W. Pink
Twentieth-Century Christian Theologian

"God has had it on His heart to show to angels and men not only how excellent His love is, but also how terrible His wrath is."[4]
Jonathan Edwards
Eighteenth-Century Christian Theologian

PROLOGUE:
YOU, AND THE GOD WHO IS

"For I am God and there is no other;
I am God and there is no one like Me. . . ."[5]
God

God is probably not who you think He is.

That is, if you're the average professing Christian, going to your average church. Sure, you have some concept of a supreme being embedded in your consciousness—but, is your god-notion, God? The one true God? The biblical God? The God who is?

Has your pastor been faithful to the biblical text or has he relentlessly edited God's revelation in order to keep you in attendance? Has your minister purposely hidden the biblical God from you in hopes that you might like his preaching and his church a bit more than you otherwise would? Of course, if you call yourself a Christian, it's your responsibility to know whether you're sitting under a flattering, revisionist impostor or a God-called preacher. Yes, that's on you. And be assured, God has not failed to notice the kind of church you have chosen to attend.

To anyone who has ears to hear, I would simply like to say that it's time to open the Book and behold the breathtaking awe and terrifying holiness of Jehovah-God. Certainly, it is long past time in this era of low-resolution preaching and pervasive biblical illiteracy. It's time to take what He says about Himself seriously, for El Shaddai will not countenance being pushed to the periphery of a trivial, religious parody. The biblical God is, by definition, the antithesis of peripheral. He *will* be central, for He *is* central whether your preacher and denomination like it or not.

It's time to know, believe, and delight in *all* that God has revealed about Himself. For indeed, to honestly look at the unredacted God of the Bible, is to never be the same. And aren't you way past ready to go on with God? Don't you want Him to blow up your heart, soul, and mind, yet again? Don't you need to know Him, more? Obviously, if you're bored with Him, you either do not know Him or you've consciously stopped seeking Him in His Word. You've decided that what you know, or think you know, about Him fits your very comfortable, commonsense life just fine. No need to upset the status quo by going deeper. If you have left off your pursuit of Him in His Word, I caution that this is a grievous error. You *must* go on with God! You *must* tremble afresh and anew! This is an ever-present necessity for every true believer.

To be sure, God is unrepentant. He is unapologetic regarding His awful majesty and fearful greatness. He has, quite literally, gone public with the infinite fury that is irrevocably grounded in His absolute holiness and abhorrence of sin. His anger is splashed all over the pages of Scripture. He has unashamedly revealed exactly who He is for every intelligent being to behold and consider.

If you do not know that the God of the Bible is a God of fierce wrath and horrifying vengeance, you have chosen willful ignorance. Such deception may afford you some superficial peace of mind just now, but worshiping and trusting your god-notion will ultimately cost you everything—forever. For indeed, the God who is, the biblical God, has revealed Himself to be the most dangerous Being in the cosmos for all who would make themselves His enemy.

☙

"A jealous and avenging God is the LORD; The LORD is avenging and wrathful. The LORD takes vengeance on His adversaries, and He reserves wrath for His enemies. . . . Who can stand before His indignation? Who can endure the burning of His anger?"[6]
Nahum, God's Prophet

NOTES

1   Hebrews 10:31.
2   All definitions are from *The American Heritage Dictionary* (Boston: Houghton Mifflin Co., 1985).
3   A. W. Pink, *The Attributes of God* (Grand Rapids MI: Baker Book House, 1995), 54.
4   Jonathan Edwards, *Sinners in the Hands of an Angry God* (New Kensington PA: Whitaker House 1997), 52.
5   Isaiah 46:9.
6   Nahum 1:2, 6.

INTRODUCTION

A Dangerous Oversight

"Prepare to meet your God. . . ."[1]
Amos, God's Prophet

So, with a title and subtitle like this—no doubt we'll sell literally tens of copies!

Obviously, I'm not much interested in book sales, but I am keenly interested in worship. You know, that genuine, soul-quaking, life-and-eternity-altering kind of worship—to truly behold the biblical God in all His revealed fullness. I want to know that God. No, I need to know that God. The God who is.

I simply can't get interested in the generic caricatures of God being dispensed in the media, in world religions, and yes, even in a pseudo-church near you. I desire to know the reigning God, the God of the Bible, before whom every thinking person reflexively trembles and the whole earth spontaneously shakes.[2] My hungry and impoverished soul craves to comprehend as much of Him as is humanly possible. I aspire to join the "four living creatures"[3] and be lost in ecstatic worship—not only for the remainder of this very short life, but for the next billion eternities! Only my Creator-Redeemer God, Jesus Christ, can fill the "eternity"[4] He wired into my thirsty heart. I must have Him . . . all of Him. He is the one non-negotiable for every awakened and alive soul. I cannot and will not settle for some domesticated iteration—some denominational pseudo-christ. I can't live that small. I won't!

To the True Lover of Christ

If you're a born-again lover of Jesus Christ, the same is obviously true for you. You already delight in, and effortlessly treasure His amiable attributes. Yes, He is a God of inexhaustible love, grace, mercy, patience, and benevolence—evidenced by the fact that He has "bought"[5] your rebellious soul out of the narcissistic pit in which you used to consciously wallow. Of course, all true believers fluently exult in the unfathomable kindness God has lavished upon them!

The point I seek to make in this book is that we all *need* to immerse ourselves far more deeply in the righteous wrath and fury of God—to know and more fully understand this revealed dimension of His. This is necessary for you and me. We must comprehend Him more completely . . . more accurately. If we do not give ourselves to this quest, our worship, and thus our lives, will unavoidably reflect a rather pedestrian view of our Creator. We simply will have no life-altering sense of His infinite holiness, and, consequently, His stunning condescension and work upon the Cross. Choosing not to pursue Him in all His fullness will ultimately diminish our understanding of who He *truly* is, and, in due course, retard our faith, joy, thankfulness, repentance, humility, obedience, and zeal.

We must fully see and understand God as He has revealed Himself in the Bible. We must fear Him as He intends. We need to know Him like this. If we do not, it could rightly be said that we do not know Him at all. Considering His Self-Revelation in Scripture, this "not knowing" can only be characterized as wholesale neglect on our part. This carelessness will perpetually redound to our spiritual poverty. For indeed, it is both "proper and excellent"[6] that we would know, love, and feast upon all that God is. We must. This is an enduring reality for every true disciple.

Our Comprehensive, Default Premise

Upon reflection, it has occurred to me that no one ever forthrightly taught me how urgently important this is—in short, to properly tremble before my Creator. And then, to bring that trembling down into the minutiae of everyday life. We're all taught the right words—yes, He is an awesome, fearsome, consuming-fire God! But knowing the words and genuinely "feeling" their heart-shaking reality deep within our souls are two dramatically different things. I'm talking about experiencing awe in such a way that it radically alters the way we think about everything. Yes, everything.

A biblically correct view of God must become our comprehensive, default premise in every circumstance of life. This is true whether we're talking about our marriage, our singleness, our life's work, our budget, or our Internet history. God, rightly viewed, alters every aspect of our lives. It's a proper fear of the breathtaking, and yes, dangerous God who made us. It's the overarching truth I've learned in writing this book. Truly, I see it as a priceless gift from God to learn to fear Him as He has purposed and commanded. Nothing is ever quite the same when you see Him as He has revealed Himself—a God of infinite wrath, vengeance, recompense, and terror. Once He has been seen in His fullness, the thoughtful person can never go back to business as usual. Never.

The Disciple's Supreme Discipline

By simple observation of the Christian community at large, it seems that we're supposed to merely tolerate God's less genial attributes, i.e., His holy anger, fury, and rage; speaking to these characteristics only when thoroughly cornered in a Bible study. I have come to see this as a more-than-subtle form of blasphemy that enfeebles the true believer's quest to rightly and entirely worship our Creator. Christian, God is who He is. He is utterly unapologetic. Yes, in His immutable holiness, righteousness, and justice, He hates sin and His fierce anger burns against the creature's insurgency. I have only recently come to fully apprehend the fact that I was designed and redeemed to *deeply* treasure these unchanging qualities of God.

As I've persisted in reading the Bible over the last three and a half decades, I've continually encountered passage after passage bluntly pressing home these attributes. We must not only learn God *correctly*, we must also learn Him *fully*. It is the supreme discipline of every authentic disciple—to never stop looking at all of Him in all of His Word! For God expects His people to both understand and, without hesitation, heartily echo the psalmist's cry of worship, "O LORD, God of vengeance; God of vengeance shine forth! Rise up, O Judge of the earth; render recompense to the proud."[7] If this God, the God of the Bible, is in full view, men and angels have only two viable options—worship or flee! This is what God intends every one of His moral creatures to comprehend in the deepest core of their being.

To the Nominal Churchgoer

If you're a nominal Christian that sometimes attends a breezy-it's-mostly-all-about-you church, you have no idea what the words wrath, vengeance, recompense, and terror have to do with you or your denominational god. These words are utterly alien to your concept of god. Your god would never threaten wrath—he's too loving. Your god would never talk vengeance—he's too forgiving. Your god would never mention recompense. Seriously, what does that even mean to someone like you with a god like yours? I mean, come on; you prayed the prayer. You did the ordinance. You're a proper church member and you try to attend church whenever it's not too inconvenient. Plus, you really are a pretty nice person.

It is, of course, utterly shocking and completely outrageous to infer that your god would ever use the word terror in relation to you or anyone else! How could that even be possible? Most assuredly, it couldn't be, right? You've been repeatedly told by your minister, and that devotional book someone gave you some years ago, as well as what you've gleaned from the culture at large, that your god loves you and has a wonderful plan for your life. Obviously, your god is crazy about you! What else could you possibly need to know? Yes, eat, drink, hoard up a bunch of cash and retire well, for your god is an easygoing, compliant, and ultimately very useful deity. He's like a real big, best friend forever.

Well, what you need to know is what your preacher has not been telling you. Your minister is either incompetent, self-serving, cowardly, or wicked. Possibly, all the above, but that's his problem, not yours. And yes, he will taste this book's subtitle up close and personal. Your problem is that you're not worshiping the God who is. You're worshiping an abridged god. A truncated god. A facsimile. A cartoon. An impotent, effeminate, neutered god. He is the pseudo-christian-god taking millions of "luke-warm"[8] churchgoers to hell. You know, the kind of professing Christians who will inevitably hear those cataclysmic words from the lips of Jesus Christ that your preacher never failed to omit from his sermon—"I never knew you, depart from Me. . . ."[9] If those words are ever addressed to you, I assure you that you will fully and inescapably comprehend wrath, vengeance, recompense, and terror. You will have an exhaustive, intensive, eternal, and infinite understanding of those words so often spoken in the Bible by the God who is.

Defending My Subtitle
So back to that subtitle no one likes. For the record, in the NASB English translation of the Bible, which is the most literal English translation from the original languages, we find by my count:

Wrath—Appearing 124 times in relation to God and His judgment.

Vengeance—Appearing 37 times in relation to God and His judgment.

Recompense—Appearing 20 times in relation to God and His judgment.

Terror—Appearing 51 times in relation to God and His judgment.

These are not unusual, isolated, exotic, hard-to-find, out-of-context themes. God repeatedly uses these words in relation to Himself and His righteous response to mankind's rebellion. This is who God has revealed Himself to be. If you profess to be a Christian and don't know this—you don't know the biblical God and you're likely sitting in a false church, under a false teacher.

Yawning at God
American theologian Michael Horton is right, "Nobody today seems to think that God is dangerous. And that is itself a dangerous oversight."[10] Amen! In brilliant fashion, *Desiring God* senior writer Tony Reinke adds that this,

> . . . is dangerous because before we yawn at God, we must first replace . . . and domesticate [Him]. . . . Who wants a God who roars, threatens, who judges? Why not rather fashion a god in our taste—a friendly god we can pet, leash, and export for popular appeal?[11]

You know, a god who works within our very own personally concocted worldview. A comfortable god we can properly manage. Of course, this is the pliable god of apostate Christianity. To be sure, there are many mysteries in the Bible—God's righteous anger, which burns against His rebellious creatures, is not one of them. If you claim to be a Christian, stop apologizing for God's holiness, His hatred of sin, and His fierce wrath. To do so is one thing and one thing only—an insult to the very dangerous God who is.

Born-again Christian: Come and Worship
So, true believer, in this book I call you to a profoundly deeper place with Jesus Christ that you might know Him more fully and worship Him more completely. In doing so, He will radically transform your life, yet again. It is my prayer that you will learn to tremble with utter, perfect, complete humility, reverence, and joy at who He is. This more fully informed and felt awe will inevitably seep into every corner of your life. This is good—very, very good. Allow me to say it yet one more time—a more biblically precise view of God will alter the way you live every single day for the rest of your life. So, lover and follower of Christ, come and worship as we dive deep into His Self-Revelation! And yes, as always, be changed afresh and anew as you learn to fear Him with perfect delight! For indeed, fear and gladness coexist in every regenerate heart![12]

Lukewarm Christian: Repent and Believe

And nominal Christian, in this book I call you to repent from your suicidal indifference toward the biblical God. You must put down your pseudo-christian god and your denominational affections and run to the God "who dwells in unapproachable light"[13] for the salvation of your soul. Pseudo-Christianity will not save you from this justly incensed God. You must be reconciled to the God who is—the God of the Bible. You must begin to know, love, worship, and obey the biblical Jesus. For the same is true of millions today that was true of the merely religious in Christ's day. Jesus told them that they worshiped God in vain, honoring Him only with their lips, keeping their hearts far from Him.[14] No thinking person engages in that kind of lethal behavior before the dangerous God of the Bible.

Casual church attender, I implore you to quit your false-christ! Come! Genuinely repent of your lethargy and truly believe on the biblical Jesus, that you "might have life and might have it abundantly!"[15] For God is unambiguous; He is not interested in your feigned commitment to Him—in fact, He detests it. Indeed, as His psalmist writes, "Those who hate the LORD would pretend obedience to Him; and their time of punishment would be forever."[16] Yes, that's a long time. Yes, those are the stakes.

An Opening Exhortation

God has clearly revealed that He is "dreadfully provoked"[17] by the premeditated and unrestrained revolt of His creatures. That's right, by your sin and mine. God's prophet, writes:

> Wail, for the day of the LORD is near! It will come as destruction from the Almighty. Therefore, all hands will fall limp and every man's heart will melt. They will be terrified. . . . Behold, the day of the LORD is coming, cruel, with fury and burning with anger. . . . The heavens will tremble, and the earth will be shaken from its place at the fury of the LORD of hosts in the day of His burning anger.[18]

It's time to know and fear this God, for we will all stand before Him soon. There will be no domesticated, user-friendly, politically correct, god-caricature sitting on the "throne"[19] on that last day—it will be the exceedingly dangerous God of the Bible: the God who has not failed to communicate the fact that He "hates all who do iniquity."[20] Every human being will stand before this God. The "terrifyingly magnificent"[21] God of unsearchable greatness before whom the whole earth trembles and the mountains melt like wax.[22] This is the God to whom we will each give an account. This holy God will be plaintiff, prosecutor, judge, and jury and, there will be no objections, counter arguments, cross-examinations, or appeals.

If you have never trembled before the risen, reigning, omnipotent, sovereign Son of God, you have clearly never met Him. And it is not hyperbole to say that you desperately need to know, that you must tremble before Him. You must have an awesome Savior. For without the biblical Jesus, the omnipotent fury and wrath of God that is so painstakingly revealed in the Bible will land on you everlastingly.

I invite you to join me in this journey through God's Word that we might know our Creator-God more correctly, fully, and deeply. This is urgent beyond description for every one of us. We must know and be reconciled to the God who is . . . the dangerous God of the Bible.

☡

"The sorrows of those who have bartered for another god will be multiplied. . . ."[23]
David, God's Psalmist

NOTES

1 Amos 4:12.
2 Psalm 99:1.
3 Revelation 4:8.
4 Ecclesiastes 3:11.
5 1 Corinthians 6:20.
6 Serno, Dwight, *The Works of President Edwards*, Volume 8. (Leeds, England: G & C & H Carvill, 1811), 392.
7 Psalm 94:1-2.
8 Revelation 3:16.
9 Matthew 7:23.
10 Tony Reinke, "Stop Apologizing for God," Desiring God Website, October 25, 2014, accessed July 10, 2016, https://www.desiringgod.org/articles/stop-apologizing-for-god.
11 Ibid.
12 Psalm 2:11.
13 1 Timothy 6:16.
14 Matthew 15:8-9.
15 John 10:10.
16 Psalm 81:15.
17 Jonathan Edwards, *Sinners in the Hands of an Angry God* (New Kensington PA: Whitaker House 1997), 31.
18 Isaiah 13:6-13 (excerpts).
19 Isaiah 6:1.
20 Psalm 5:5.
21 John Piper, *Spectacular Sins* (Wheaton, IL: Crossway, 2008), 13.
22 Job 37:22, Isaiah 2:19, Hebrews 12:21 Hebrews 12:29, Psalms 145:3, Psalms 97:4-5.
23 Psalm 16:4.

one

3 TIMES HOLY

God's Unapproachable Otherness

"Woe is me, for I am ruined!"[1]
Isaiah, God's Prophet

Why Isaiah's impassioned lament?

Why was he, a prophet's prophet who was likely more righteous than any of his contemporaries, ruined? Why this cry of despair? Why this self-indictment of damnation? Why this sudden, gut-wrenching epiphany?

Because God granted him an unencumbered glimpse of Himself.

And with that vision of the "King of glory"[2] on His throne, Isaiah immediately knew two things were inescapably true—God is holy, and he was not. This is the real life, calamitous condition of every human being. And this, if not remedied, will result in each one of us meeting God as an enemy. Obviously, this would be eternally catastrophic. Indeed, according to the clear teaching of the Bible, this would be eternal "woe." It would be omnipotent wrath, vengeance, recompense, and terror forever . . . the unavoidable outworking of provoked Holiness!

No More Pleasant Fictions

Of course, Isaiah knew God was holy, at least intellectually. It was Jewish doctrine and history. But now, he has glimpsed God and his abstract notions of what holy meant had been obliterat-

26

ed. Instantaneously, God's holiness was a heart-quaking, fear-some, and trembling reality. Other English translations of the Bible put the words "undone, lost, doomed, and destroyed" in Isaiah's mouth. For the first time in his life, he had some genuine insight into the awesome God who is. And consequently, for the first time in his life, he had some small awareness of the horrific nature of his sin. He fully and deeply perceived the gaping chasm his personal iniquity had created between himself and his Holy-Creator. No more pleasant fictions about who he thought he was before Yahweh. No more divine misconceptions. No more religious delusions. Now, there was no doubt; he was hopelessly exposed. In an instant, his rather high opinion of himself was destroyed. He experienced, as American theologian R. C. Sproul writes, "pure moral anguish, the kind that rips out the heart of a man and tears his soul to pieces . . . [as] relentless guilt screamed from his every pore."[3] Isaiah now knew without doubt that he was exhaustively ruined—from the inside out. This is what it's like for a human being to come face-to-face with the God who is.

Isaiah's Problem is Your Problem

Yeah, I know you've got problems. Lots of them, right? Problems with your job. Problems with your family. Problems with your budget, and your neighbor, and your dog, and your lawn, etc., etc., etc. But Isaiah's problem is, in fact, your most urgent and grave problem—God is holy and you're not. All your other problems pale in comparison. They are temporal and will all soon be six feet under with your corpse. The God-is-holy-and-you're-not problem will transcend your dignified funeral. Indeed, it will define every second of your eternity. You and I are just like Isaiah in this regard. In the face of Holiness, we are utterly and wholly ruined—everlastingly doomed! If you don't know that this is true, you've not yet genuinely encountered the biblical God. The God of Scripture. The God Isaiah saw. The God who reflexively evokes the word "woe" deep within the human soul. The God before whom, no one ever yawns. The dangerous God.

The Involuntary Genuflect

The Bible records that every man who was granted a glimpse of the awesome, overpowering, yes, crushing holiness of God, as Isaiah did, was similarly affected:

> **Moses** "hid his face, for he was afraid to look at God."[4]
> **Joshua** "fell on his face to the earth."[5]
> **Ezekiel** "fell on [his] face. . . . "[6]
> **Daniel's** "color turned to a deathly pallor and [he] retained no strength . . . with [his] face to the ground."[7]
> **Peter, James,** and **John** "fell on their faces and were much afraid."[8]
> **Paul** "fell to the ground. . . . "[9]
> And **John** again, in receiving the Revelation, "fell . . . as a dead man."[10]

These are the instinctive, seemingly involuntary responses of God's prophets and apostles when confronted with His overwhelming supernatural, personal presence. Again, these men are way more holy than you and I, yet they unquestioningly knew that, before the blazing presence of God, they were anything but holy. They, too, were "undone." Canadian pastor Tim Challies is spot on when he writes, "The basic human condition is to believe that God isn't really all that holy and that I'm not really that bad. . . . So we are a good match, God and I."[11] This is a miscalculation of infinite and everlasting proportions. King David prayed correctly "For in Your sight no man living is righteous."[12] Compared to God, human righteousness is, as Isaiah writes, "like a filthy garment."[13] Translation: "like menstrual cloths."[14] This is a reality that every human being will ultimately and eternally understand.

Holiness Defined

Clearly, we need to understand just what is being said about God as the thrice-holy Sovereign of heaven and earth.[15] What is this unique attribute of God from which wrath, vengeance, recompense, and terror lavishly flow? The dictionary tells us:

Holy *adj.* 1. Belonging to, derived from, or associated with a divine power; sacred. 2. Regarded with or worthy of worship or veneration; revered. . . . 3. . . . .Highly moral. . . . 4. . . . .Set apart.[16]

His Power

As the first meaning discloses, holiness is unavoidably linked with the divine which, of course, implies deific power. As the Bible relentlessly reveals, Yahweh is not wanting in this regard. Scripture tells us that He simply spoke a two trillion galaxy cosmos, with a known diameter of 93 billion light years, into existence. This is a breathtakingly stunning exhibition of transcendent might. And yes, this is the "hiding of His power"[17] as the prophet alludes! Yes, Creation is the hiding of His power. Think about it. This is reason enough to cause prophets and apostles to hide their faces in the presence of One who possess primal omnipotence!

His Magnificence

Infinite power yields the oh-so-apparent deduction that such a Being is worthy of the absolute worship and reverence of the creature as the second meaning noted suggests. Again, this is self-evidently true as seen in the spontaneous responses of the men listed above who were granted an unimpeded vision of their Creator. There was no lethargy in their veneration. It was traumatically necessary, immediate, and mandatory to get as low as possible, as quickly as possible. It's what the unholy urgently *needs* to do in the face of the Holy.

His Purity

The third meaning above flows effortlessly from our mental lexicon. If holy means anything, it must mean perfect, unsullied, absolute purity, virtuousness, goodness, integrity, honesty, decency, and righteousness. The biblical God is "the antithesis of all moral blemish or defilement."[18] He is righteous, and therefore can do none other than what is pristinely right. His unrivalled righteousness, the obvious outworking of holiness, immutably flows from His faultless character and nature. The unholy must, and does, recoil in abject dread of invincible moral purity.

His Otherness

And the fourth meaning noted amplifies a core reason for Isaiah's heart-rending self-indictment at the sight of I AM. It is a fundamental meaning of holy in the Isaiah text. God is set apart, distinct, separate, other, foreign. Of course, if He is God, He is, by definition, infinitely above, outside, and beyond His creation. The Scriptures reveal that the supernatural otherness of God evokes an impulsive terror in the heart of mankind. Again, Sproul writes:

> When we encounter Him, the totality of our creatureliness breaks upon us and shatters the myth that we have believed about ourselves, the myth that we are demigods, junior-grade deities who will try to live forever. . . . God is too great for us; He is too awesome. . . . In His presence we quake and tremble. Meeting Him personally may be our greatest trauma.[19]

There is nothing more true in all creation than the fact that apart from a saving relationship with Jesus Christ, meeting God *will be* our greatest trauma—an everlasting and infinite trauma!

Attribute of Attributes

God's Self-revelation is awash in His holy-otherness. In the NASB translation, the word *holy* or *holiness* appears no fewer than 583 times. According to my count, 244 of those occurrences are in direct reference to God. The remaining instances refer to people, places, and things set apart by God for His purposes. Considering mankind's inbred aversion to the holy and the Bible's incessant references to it, twentieth-century theologian A. W. Pink properly asserts that this "clearly demonstrates [the] superhuman origin" of the Scriptures. He continues, "An ineffably holy God, who has the utmost abhorrence of all sin, was never invented by any of Adam's fallen descendants!"[20]

Isaiah heard the seraphim call out to his colleague, "Holy, Holy, Holy, is the LORD of hosts. The whole earth is full of His glory."[21] John heard a similar refrain from the four living creatures in the Revelation. "Holy, Holy, Holy, is the Lord God the

Almighty, who was and who is and who is to come."[22] In the Bible, no other attribute of God is used in this way. As a thrice echoed appellation of worship from creature to Creator. This passionate, full-throated angelic worship is utterly unique. We do not see such worship built around any of God's other manifold characteristics. To borrow from Sproul again, there is no biblical chorus of "'love, love, love' or 'mercy, mercy, mercy' or 'wrath, wrath, wrath' or 'justice, justice, justice,'"[23] recorded in God's Word. The hosts of heaven are letting us know what *the* transcendent attribute of God is; His holy-otherness. This quality defines and informs all others. It is "an attribute of attributes!"[24] These captivated angelic beings are acknowledging and proclaiming what every creature viscerally knows: "There is no One like You! There is no One like You! There is no one like You!" He is, without question, the incomparable, unapproachable Other!

Isaiah's God Is God

It can be no coincidence that after Isaiah's vision, he wrote some of the loftiest prose in all the Bible regarding the supernatural otherness of God. It is the unyielding chorus of Isaiah chapters 40 through 46 where God unapologetically states that He is God and nobody else is! Yes, the biblical God is other. He is the unrivaled Uncreated, the unequaled Unbegun. Twentieth-century Christian apologist C. S. Lewis says it pretty well: "In the long run God is no one but Himself and what He does is like nothing else. You could hardly expect it to be."[25]

God inquires, "To whom then will you liken Me that I should be his equal?"[26] It's what every thinking person inherently grasps—at least in the abstract. There is no one like Him! It is in fact what Moses, Joshua, Isaiah, Ezekiel, Daniel, Peter, James, John, and Paul learned firsthand. It was no longer theoretical. They learned this reality in their reflexive face-down-as-quickly-as-is-humanly-possible encounters with Elohim. Regarding God's transcendent otherness, Isaiah writes

> Behold, the nations are like a drop from a bucket, and are regarded as a speck of dust on the scales. . . . All the nations are as nothing before Him, they are regarded by

Him as less than nothing and meaningless. To whom
then will you liken God? It is He who sits above the vault
of the earth, and all the inhabitants are like grasshoppers.[27]

It's a really good idea for us to think deeply about Isaiah's
words here. He says that, before God, the earth's inhabitants are
like "grasshoppers" and the nations are as a "speck of dust." Does
that not give you at least some small sense of scale relative to you
and the indefinable, transcendent otherness of the "Alpha and
the Omega, the first and the last, the beginning and the end"[28]
God? Yes, again, the thoughtful person must worship or flee!

Lethal Holiness
Indeed, who would trifle with Isaiah's God? I mean, who plays
games with the you-cannot-see-My-face-and-live God?[29] Who in
their right mind would be high-handed before the God of Moses
and what would be the just consequences of such insanity? The
foregoing *who* questions are merely rhetorical devices meant to
emphasize the utter stupidity of that kind of conduct. But as to
the question concerning God's righteous reaction toward those
who are insolent before Him, He does not leave us guessing.
While it is rare that God's justice is immediately visible—as we
will witness in the following four biblical accounts—it is always
and finally inevitable. Holiness is always toxic to the unholy.
Every day it is lethal to defy holy God, and His response comes
solely at His discretion. It may be immediate as we will see from
the pages of Scripture. Or, it may come to us at the end of a long,
healthy, prosperous, pseudo-Christian life. As I will repeat several times throughout this book, life and death are always God's
business. It would be wise for each of us to receive God's unmistakably clear message from the following narratives.

Holiness and Dereliction
They were Aaron's sons. They were priests. They knew the job.
They knew what God expected. It wasn't difficult. It wasn't com-
plicated. You know, just have enough conviction to be competent.
Just follow straightforward, easy to understand directions. Just

simply do what the "God of heaven"[30] had commanded. No more, no less. But Nadab and Abihu couldn't seem to be bothered with merely doing what God had instructed them to do. Inexplicably, they offered "strange fire before the LORD, which He had not commanded them."[31]

And how did Holiness respond? "And fire came out from the presence of the LORD and consumed them, and they died before the LORD."[32] No trial. No hearing. No extenuating evidence. No debate. No excuses. No appeal. Just a divine execution. Was it right? Was it just? Yes, God did it! That makes it right! That makes it just! Was this a divine overreaction? No! It was the presumptuous unholy behaving badly in the very presence of the provoked Holy! That can only ever end one way—the way it ended for these two guys. God says, "By those who come near Me I will be treated as holy, and before all the people I will be honored." So, the text tells us that "Aaron kept silent."[33] Every unholy mouth is shut before the Holy! Perfect justice was not only immediately rendered; it was immediately seen as right. David sings this truth for the whole world to know, understand, and never forget—that when God judges, He is "blameless."[34]

Holiness and Defiance

He was the great-grandson of Levi. His name was Korah. He and his mates decided to take on God's man, Moses. He openly and defiantly challenged God's chosen prophet. Then the LORD told Moses to have the congregation "get back from around the dwellings of Korah, Dathan and Abiram."[35] Not a good sign for the conspirators. The Bible records that . . .

> the earth opened its mouth and swallowed them up and their households, and all the men who belonged to Korah, with their possessions. So, they and all that belonged to them went down alive to Sheol; and the earth closed over them, and they perished from the midst of the assembly.[36]

The text continues, "Fire also came forth from the LORD and consumed the two hundred and fifty men who were"[37] part of the rebellion. Unbelievably, the next day, there were those among the Hebrews who "grumbled" against Moses for the carnage in the camp. Immediately, the wrath of God went forth and 14,700 more died.[38] What is the unavoidable takeaway? Holiness tolerates no defiance. Again, we see that perfect justice was immediately delivered. It is important to never forget that this is the prerogative of Holy-Other every minute of every day—to violently take out the defiant!

Holiness and Disobedience

God had brought the exodus Jews into the Promised Land and told Joshua that with only a little marching, a little blowing of trumpets, and a little shouting, Jericho would be theirs. And, so it was. But God had warned the people that "all the silver and gold and articles of bronze and iron are holy to the LORD [and] shall go into the treasury of the LORD."[39] Achan decided he would simply ignore God's command and keep some booty for himself. No harm done, right? God's got a lot of stuff. He won't notice what I've stolen from Him. Yeah, that's the thing about God, He knows. He knows it all. He knows our "thoughts"[40] and the "word"[41] before it's on our tongues. You can be sure that "your sin will find you out."[42] It found Achan out. The text tells us that "the anger of the LORD burned."[43] Joshua writes that he and all of Israel with him took Achan and all that he had stolen and

> his sons, his daughters, his oxen, his donkeys, his sheep, his tent and all that belonged to him; and they brought them up to the valley of Achor. . . . And all Israel stoned them with stones; and they burned them with fire after they had stoned them with stones.[44]

As the rebellious sin of Achan was mercilessly rooted out and righteously dealt with in accordance with the command of God, the text says, ". . .and the LORD turned from the fierceness of His anger."[45] What is the universal consequence of rebellion in the Bible? It's always the same. The holy and fierce anger and wrath of a dangerous God.

Holiness and Duplicity

Absolutely everyone was on board. "Not one"[46] claimed otherwise as they were liquidating assets and laying the proceeds at the apostles' feet[47] in order to meet the needs of the impoverished among them. There was great excitement and joy in the congregation as they enthusiastically decided to hold all things in common.[48] Ananias and his wife Saphira had obviously agreed to do the same. They, too, sold some property but, the text tells us, held a portion back for themselves. Perfectly legitimate, except for the fact that they had clearly consented to the congregational pact. Peter asked, "Why has Satan filled your heart to lie to the Holy Spirit . . . [and] put the Spirit to the test? You have not lied to men, but to God."[49] Ananias and Saphira were struck down by God and died on the spot "and great fear came upon the whole church."[50] It was a breathtaking exhibition of incited Holiness. An unforgettable lesson for the fledgling church. The Christian God is God, and He is holy. He hates spiritual pretense and religious duplicity. This is invariably true in the Bible—man's presumption is always met with divine indignation.

Shocking!

The foregoing accounts are more than a little shocking to those who are not intimate with the Word of God. However, what is truly astonishing throughout Scripture is not that God occasionally renders immediate judgment upon those who are defiant toward Him, but that He is routinely so longsuffering with the rest of us. The wise king speaks to mankind's penchant to presume on the patience of God. Solomon writes, "Because the sentence against an evil deed is not executed quickly, therefore the hearts of the sons of men among them are given fully to do evil."[51] The world is saturated with obstinate men "given fully" to live unholy lives under the gaze of the Holy. This is idiocy of the highest order. God's apostle warns:

> . . .do you think lightly of the riches of His kindness and forbearance and patience, not knowing that the kindness of God leads you to repentance? But because of your stubbornness and unrepentant heart you are storing up

wrath for yourself in the day of wrath and revelation of the righteous judgment of God, who will render to every man according to His deeds.[52]

The holy justice that was immediately issued forth upon Nadab, Abihu, Korah and his co-conspirators, as well as Achan, and Ananias and Saphira will ultimately befall every insubordinate soul. These accounts reveal ultimate reality. They shock us because we are not well versed in ultimate reality. That's on us, for God has faithfully revealed His holy otherness to us in His Word.

Forever Consequences

God means for you to not only be aware of Isaiah's problem but to understand it. God means for you to feel Isaiah's "woe" for that is who you and I really are before Him. God is holy and we are not. God's Self-revelation has made it clear: the Holy is dangerous to the unholy. Wrath, vengeance, recompense, and terror are the forever consequences of provoked Holiness. God has said it. He has warned us. He has done it historically, and He has promised to do it again. The Scriptures render more than a few accounts of the thrice holy God's resolve in this regard.

✍

"Who will not fear, O Lord, and glorify Your name?
For You alone are holy. . . . "[53]
John, God's Apostle

NOTES

1   Isaiah 6:5.
2   Psalm 24:10.
3   R. C. Sproul, *The Holiness of God* (Carol Stream, IL: Tyndale Momentum, 1998), 30.
4   Exodus 3:6.
5   Joshua 5:14.
6   Ezekiel 1:28.
7   Daniel 10:8-9.
8   Matthew 17:6.
9   Acts 9:3-4.
10   Revelation 1:17.
11   Tim Challies, "God's Not Really That Holy, I'm Not Really That Bad" Challies. com, November 9, 2015, accessed August 15, 2019, https://www.challies.com/articles/gods-not-really-that-holy-im-not-really-that-bad/.
12   Psalm 143:2.
13   Isaiah 64:6.
14   John MacArthur, *The John MacArthur Study Bible* (Nashville, TN: Word Publishing, 1997), Footnote on Isaiah 64:6.
15   Isaiah 6:3.
16   "Holy," *The American Heritage Dictionary* (Boston: Houghton Mifflin Co., 1985).
17   Habakkuk 3:4.
18   A. W. Pink, *The Attributes of God* (Grand Rapids MI: Baker Book House, 1995), 41.
19   Sproul, 44.
20   Pink, 44.
21   Isaiah 6:3.
22   Revelation 4:8.
23   Sproul, 25.
24   Pink, 42.
25   C. S. Lewis, *A Year with C. S. Lewis* (New York, NY: HarperCollins Publishers, 2003), 140.
26   Isaiah 40:25.
27   Isaiah 40:15-22, (excerpts).
28   Revelation 22:13.
29   Exodus 33:20.
30   Psalm 136:26.
31   Leviticus 10:1.
32   Leviticus 10:2.
33   Leviticus 10:3.
34   Psalm 51:4.
35   Numbers 16:24.
36   Numbers 16:32-33.
37   Numbers 16:35.
38   Numbers 16:46-49.
39   Joshua 6:19.
40   Ezekiel 11:5.
41   Psalm 139:4.
42   Numbers 32:23.
43   Joshua 7:1.
44   Joshua 7:24-25.
45   Joshua 7:26.
46   Acts 4:32.
47   Acts 4:34-35.
48   Acts 4:32.
49   Acts 5:3-9.
50   Acts 5:5,10-11.
51   Ecclesiastes 8:11.
52   Romans 2:4-6.
53   Revelation 15:4.

two

1 Sin

God's Just Response

"Cursed is the ground because of you. . . . "[1]
God

Why all this mayhem and calamity in the world? Why all this suffering? Why all this personal tragedy? Why all these natural disasters? Why all this sickness and deformity? Why murder? Why pornography? Why false religion? Why terrorists? Why all this brokenness and heartache? Why all these wars? Why all this death?

Because of one sin. Just one.

One sin brought down paradise. One sin. Just one. One sin subjected a two-trillion galaxy cosmos to corruption.[2] One sin. I want you to feel the weight and catastrophic scope of that. It was one sin. One sin. One sin against one God. The infinitely holy God who is. With one sin, mankind declared his independence from God, unleashing the knowledge of evil and, consequently, the just wrath, vengeance, recompense, and terror of Yahweh. One sin. Why is the world messed up? It's not because God is messed up; it's because we messed up. The Bible is clear, we sinned in Adam.[3] I know, some don't like the doctrine of original sin. Again, what always matters is not whether you like a biblical assertion or not, but whether God has said it. That's all that ultimately matters. And yes, God has pointedly revealed this truth. So, with one sin *we* let loose the horrors of evil and God's inevi-

38

table and righteous response.

We rebelled against our Creator—knowingly, and with premeditation. We ate of the "tree of the knowledge of good and evil"[4] and we have "reaped the whirlwind"[5] of unrestrained wickedness and, yes, God's omnipotent fury ever since. Why all the evil in the world? We set that in motion by turning our backs on God. We are a damned species living on a condemned planet that is "reserved for fire."[6] One sin did that as we tasted evil and the thrice-holy God unfailingly responded with perfect justice. The God who is, hates sin and, as His psalmist reminds us, "is a righteous judge . . . who has indignation every day."[7]

Defining Sin

What is the meaning of this word the modern culture has ruthlessly sought to expunge from common parlance? The dictionary tells us:

> Sin *n.* 1. A transgression of a religious or moral law, esp. when deliberate. 2. A condition of estrangement from God as a result of breaking God's law. 3. An offense, violation, fault, or error.[8]

This secular definition is, shall we say, utterly inadequate from a biblical perspective. The definition is simply too sedate, too sterile. Sin is not merely breaking a law and consequently being estranged from God. Sin is the creature's white-hot rebellion against his Creator. Sin is not an "error." It is more akin to a frenzied insurgence. In Scripture, sin is always personal. It's always personal with I AM. Sin is a personal affront to a personal God. And as the apostle tells us, it's personal from mankind's perspective as well. What has fallen man done? He has not merely chosen indifference toward God; he has preferred to become a hater of God.[9] It doesn't get much more personal than that. Indeed, man has exchanged the truth of God for a lie. He refuses to acknowledge God any longer.[10] This antipathy between God and man is the consequence of man's shocking decision to rebel against a benevolent Sovereign. Make no mistake, every sin is personal. It's between you and an incensed God—every time.

Suicidal Insanity

Sin is, to paraphrase contemporary American theologian John Piper, the suicidal exchange of the glory of God for sugar-coated substitutes. Why does any thinking person do this? It's truly hard to figure. There is something mysteriously dark, gloomy, macabre, and sinister in the fallen, rebellious nature of man. He enthusiastically runs to soulish destruction. He keeps company with the spiritually bankrupt and he does so with unflinching abandon. God calls the heavens to be appalled at such lunacy.

> Has a nation changed gods, when they were not gods? But My people have changed their glory for that which does not profit. "Be appalled, O heavens, at this, and shudder, be very desolate" declares the LORD. "For My people have committed two evils: They have forsaken Me, the fountain of living waters, to hew for themselves cisterns, broken cisterns that can hold no water."[11]

This is the ultimate cosmic outrage. The supreme essence of evil. Eschewing God and preferring someone or something over Him. It is, as the prophet says, a forsaking of God to pursue some temporal pleasure that can never satisfy the insatiable spiritual thirst within the soul of man. God likens this psychosis to drinking from a dry well. Mankind has shown that he is willing to exchange his soul at "Vanity Fair"[12] for just about anything. From success to . . . family, comfort, fine houses, acclaim, positions, games, politics, fictitious news, sexual perversion, fashionable religion, etc., etc., etc., *ad nauseam*. It's a not-so-subtle "No Thank You!" to the One who designed, created, and made bountiful provision for us. It quite naturally raises the question—How did we ever get to this unbelievably stupid and self-destructive place?

A Utopian Wonderland

They had everything! Everything! Abundant food and provision in a garden paradise. They had satisfying work. They had human love and sexual pleasure. They had joy, wonder, and unbridled expectations for the future. There was only beauty, peace, well-being, and prosperity there, all day, every day. Moreover, they were created holy from the hand of a holy God with whom they had unencumbered fellowship. There was only one command. Just one. This wasn't hard. In fact, God could not have made it any easier for Adam and Eve to remain holy. He aggressively stacked the deck in our favor. There were not ten prohibitions, or five, or even two. There was one. They were not to partake of the "tree."[13] Everything, and yes that means everything north, south, east, and west of that tree was theirs to have, consume, and enjoy. A utopian wonderland with but one restriction. By anyone's standards, this was doable. In fact, it was a lay-up. I mean how could we mess this up, right?

Enter Satan

Who is this serpent in the garden?[14] Ezekiel tells us that this being was the blameless, anointed cherub dwelling on the holy mountain of God, possessing the seal of perfection, wisdom, and beauty until unrighteousness was found in him and God cast him to the ground.[15] Conservative theologians agree that Ezekiel 28 reaches behind the king of Tyre to the supernatural source of evil, Satan—the angelic dissident. He is the origin of rebellion. The prophets recount his fall:

> Your heart was lifted up because of your beauty; you corrupted your wisdom by reason of your splendor. . . . You were internally filled with violence, and you sinned. . . . You said in your heart, "I will ascend to heaven; I will raise my throne above the stars of God. . . . I will ascend above the height of the clouds; I will make myself like the Most High."[16]

The Inevitable Question

We've all heard the question, have we not? Namely, if God is both good and omnipotent, why is there evil? It's important to note that according to the summation of the creation account in Genesis, evil is not a created thing. For "God saw all that He had made . . . was very good."[17] The Scriptures clearly reveal that evil arose from the free will, moral choices of the good, but mutable creatures God created. First through Satan and the mutineer angels who followed him, and then through man. The creature, created good, chose to depart from goodness—enter evil. The Bible is unequivocal on this point. The responsibility for the presence of evil in the world lands solely at the feet of the creature. I've always liked the analogies that darkness is no thing, and cold is no thing, but are merely the absence of light and heat. It could be said that evil is no thing, but the absence of love for God within the heart of the creature. Whether the analogy holds up or not, again, it is the clear biblical assertion that evil arises and metastasizes within the creature. Considering this scriptural reality, it is indeed the height of narcissistic audacity for mankind to then, in turn, point the finger at God.

Obviously, to say evil came *from* God is blasphemous. But to in turn say, evil did not come *by* God is equally blasphemous. "Evil has come *by* good but not *from* good."[18] If we are Bible believers, we understand and heartily acknowledge that God is the reigning, ruling Sovereign of heaven and earth. Nothing, including evil, is beyond His reach, authority, and control. God, while not the author of evil, obviously had good reasons for allowing evil to arise from His good creation—not least being the glory of His Son in the redemption of His people. Yeah, I know. Maybe some of you are pretty sure you could have arranged all the particulars of the created order much better than God. But I agree with contemporary American theologian Francis Chan on this one. He writes: "When you get your own universe, you can make your own standards . . . let's not assume it's [God's] reasoning that needs correction."[19] Very, very good counsel for the thinking person.

Indeed, Has God Said?

The Genesis 3 text tells us that Satan is crafty—meaning he is cunning, sneaky, shrewd, devious, and underhanded. I think you already know that about him, don't you—from personal experience? So, he comes to Eve with a question. "Indeed, has God said, 'You shall not eat from any tree of the garden?'"[20] What is this fallen angel attacking? The same thing he always attacks: the Word of God. Many have said that Eve was no match for this supernatural being. But she had all she needed. She had God's Word. All she needed to do was believe God and obey Him. She didn't.

Satan was selling what he's always sold. He's never had to change his promotional scheme. He has two basic marketing ploys that most of humanity is still buying. One—God is not good; He is holding out on us. The backhanded implication is that we're all victims. And two—Satan is always telling us that sin is better. Well, if we look at the Genesis account and subsequent human history, it's not difficult to see that we were sold a bill of goods on both counts. Reality declares that we're not victims but thankless usurpers. And in our rebellion, we've learned, first-hand, that sin is not better. Why all this mayhem and calamity in the world? We embraced that turncoat cherub's monstrous lie. We chose against God, which is the fundamental definition of evil. And in choosing evil, evil is precisely what we have inherited.

Rebellious Adjectives

God had clearly said that to eat of the forbidden fruit would mean death. It is first spiritual death—"dead in your trespasses and sins"[21] kind of death, "excluded from the life of God"[22] kind of death. And then, inescapably and inevitably, physical death. Satan told Eve that wasn't true and that, as a revolutionary, she could "be like God, knowing good and evil."[23] Yeah, he's good, isn't he? A lie wrapped in a half-truth. For indeed, she would become like God in the sense that she would now know evil. Previously, she had only known good. Now she would become intimately acquainted with evil as would her posterity. It is the fallen human condition. We know good and we know evil. As history has well documented, it was not only an iniquitous bargain, but it was a ghastly one as well.

This proposed rebellion appealed to Eve on a number of levels. It looked good. It was attractive. It was desirable. So "she took . . . and ate"[24] as did her husband. C. S. Lewis writes:

They wanted, as we say, to "call their souls their own." But that means to live a lie, for our souls are not, in fact, our

43

own. They wanted some corner in the universe of which they could say to God, "This is our business, not yours." But there is no such corner. They wanted to be nouns, but they were, and eternally must be, mere adjectives[25]

How can you not love Lewis? He was fallible like the rest of us but does have a way of cutting through to the essential nature of things. Adjectives wanting to be nouns! Yeah, every human being's aspiration since that catastrophic moment in history!

Not Even One

The Genesis text tells us that, after the fall, Adam and Eve began their earnest search for God. Hasn't every human being eagerly sought for God since that fateful day? It's not that we're not looking, it's just that He is so hard to find. Oh wait! That's not it. How does the apostle say it in Romans 3? And allow me to amplify this point just a bit, for this truth is essential in understanding who we are at the core and our deep-seated problem with Holiness. Regarding fallen man, Paul writes:

> There is none righteous, not even one; there is none who understands, there is none who seeks for God; all have turned aside together they have become useless; there is none who does good, there is not even one. Their throat is an open grave, with their tongues they keep deceiving, the poison of asps is under their lips; whose mouth is full of cursing and bitterness; their feet are swift to shed blood, destruction and misery are in their paths, and the path of peace have they not known. There is no fear of God before their eyes.[26]

This is who mankind is. This is who you are. This is who I am. All you have to do is watch the six o'clock news, read a newspaper, surf the Internet, or listen to yourself for a little while. Yes, Romans 3 is dead-on. It's what we do. Listen to the prophet: "The heart is more deceitful than all else and is desperately sick; who can understand it?"[27] Solomon writes, "The hearts of the sons of men are full of evil, and insanity is in their hearts throughout their lives. . . . ."[28] The Holy Spirit tells us that natural man, or the unregenerate, unconverted man, ". . .does not accept the things of the Spirit of God; for they are foolishness to him, and he cannot understand them because they are spiritually appraised."[29] And that, humanity is, "hostile toward God."[30]

So, let's dispense with the mythology that mankind wants God and is searching for Him but just can't find Him. We, as Adam's descendants, are exactly like him in this regard. We're hiding like Adam . . . because we are Adam. We know we are naked. We know we are exposed. We know we have transgressed the Word of God, and we know that God knows. And while some may acquiesce to a little religion on Sunday, the very last thing many genuinely want to do is encounter the biblical God. Mankind is exactly like our first father and mother, hiding in the proverbial bushes. It's why pseudo-churches are full of people—all hiding from God in the most inconspicuous place.

Where Are You?

Maybe the most beautiful question in all human history—God said to Adam, "Where are you?"[31] Even in our premeditated rebellion, God came for us. God initiates. God seeks, that He may save. Yes, His righteous judgment upon our wanton mutiny will ultimately bring down the whole cosmos, but there is also provision made for any and all who would repent and believe. More on that later in Chapter Nine. And, of course, it's not that God doesn't know where Adam is; it's that God knows that Adam doesn't know where Adam is. He is utterly lost in a metaphysical sense.

Adam comes out of hiding and God asks him, "Have you eaten from the tree of which I commanded you not to eat?"[32] Adam's a lot like you and me. He's pretty sure none of this is his fault. He believes he's a bit of a victim here. Right? I mean, why the tree? Why the prohibition? Granted there was only one command but, you know, why the one? Yeah, and why free will? Couldn't God have built a more user-friendly cosmos? And while we're on this, why this woman that *You* gave me? Unbelievably, Adam backhandedly blamed God! And as God inquired of Eve, come to find out, she was a victim too! Obviously from Eve's perspective, all this unpleasantness was the serpent's fault. It's exceedingly profitable for us all to understand the precise origin of human victimhood. It was all about a devil, and evil, and rebellion. If you think you're a victim, Satan has you right where he wants you.

Just One Sin

God judged Satan. God judged the woman. God judged the man.[33] The whole cosmos was subjected to futility and corruption.[34] And our death sentence was infallibly pronounced—we would return to the dust.[35] This was the consequence of one sin. Just one. That's how unspeakably monstrous one sin is before God. All this disorder in the universe is not some flaw in the Creator or in His handiwork. It's evidence of our guilt before God and His perfect judgment against us. Regarding calamity and suffering in the world, Piper says it about as well as it's ever been said:

> The sufferings of this life are part of a universal, God-decreed collapse of creation into disorder because of sin. God has subjected the world to futility because of sin. . . . Therefore all the misery in the world—and it is great—is a bloody declaration about the ghastly horror of sin. . . . All natural evil is a statement about the horror of moral evil. . . . Calamities are God's previews of what sin deserves and will one day receive in judgment [but] a thousand times worse. They are warnings. . . . God mercifully shouts to us in . . . calamities: Wake up! Sin is like this! Sin leads to things like this. . . . The natural world is shot through with horrors to wake us from the dream world of thinking sin is no big deal. It is a horrifically big deal.[36]

All the disorder in our world is a physical picture of the moral disorder we have willfully embraced. All calamity is a foreshadowing of the supernatural, eternal calamity awaiting every impenitent soul. God says, "I will act with wrathful hostility against you. . . . I will pour out My wrath on sin."[37] All tragedy and death are the outworking of God's wrath owing to our unending provocations aimed at our Creator.

The Inescapable Truth

So, why all this mayhem and calamity in the world? Why all this suffering? Why all this personal tragedy? Why all this natural disaster? Why all this sickness and deformity? Why murder? Why pornography? Why false religion? Why terrorists? Why all this brokenness and heartache? Why all these wars? Why all this death? This is not a mystery. It is the consequence of one sin, and it all prefigures eternal ruin. God's visible judgment in the natural realm is warning us about the reality and severity of His promised judgment in the supernatural realm—hell—the ultimate, eternal, and infinite calamity. You and I are not victims. We are malevolent rebels who have offended a holy, almighty, and dangerous God. No, you have not misunderstood; it is as bad as it could possibly be!

One sin brought the whole cosmos down. It was one sin. Just one. A rather innocuous sin at that—simply eating what God had said not to eat. I mean, it wasn't murder or anything, right? It was just eating some fruit. But that *is* the inescapable truth here. Before God, there are no small, inoffensive sins; no matter how seemingly harmless they appear to you. Every sin is a determined act of creature rebellion—a very personal assault upon God and His authority. Each sin is heinous beyond description before perfect holiness and, yes, omnipotent fury is kindled against every single one of them. This should give each of us pause and at least some small sense of God's fixed hatred of most of what we think, feel, and do. For the thoughtful person, the question inevitably emerges—how many times have I sinned against the Holy One?

᎒

"Behold, I am against you. . . . I shall punish you according to the results of your deeds."[38]
God

NOTES

1   Genesis 3:17.
2   Romans 8:20-21.
3   Psalm 51:5, Jeremiah 17:9, Romans 5:12, 18-19, Hebrews 7:7-10.
4   Genesis 2:17, 3:6.
5   Hosea 8:7.
6   2 Peter 3:7.
7   Psalm 7:11.
8   "Sin," *The American Heritage Dictionary* (Boston: Houghton Mifflin Co., 1985).
9   Romans 1:30.
10   Romans 1:25, 28.
11   Jeremiah 2:11-13.
12   John Bunyan, *Pilgrims Progress Retold by James Thomas* (Chicago, IL: Moody Press, 1964), 89-90.
13   Genesis 2:16-17.
14   Genesis 3:1-5.
15   Ezekiel 28:12-17.
16   Ezekiel 28:16,17, Isaiah 14:13-14.
17   Genesis 1:31.
18   John Gerstner, *Handout Theology*, from Theology Video Series (Ligonier Ministries).
19   Francis Chan, *Crazy Love* (Colorado Springs, CO: David C. Cook Publishing, 2008), 34.
20   Genesis 3:1.
21   Ephesians 2:1.
22   Ephesians 4:18.
23   Genesis 3:5.
24   Genesis 3:6.
25   C. S. Lewis, *A Year With C.S. Lewis* (New York, NY: HarperCollins Publishers, 2003), 361.
26   Romans 3:10-18.
27   Jeremiah 17:9.
28   Ecclesiastes 9:3.
29   1 Corinthians 2:14.
30   Romans 8:7.
31   Genesis 3:9.
32   Genesis 3:11.
33   Genesis 3:14-19.
34   Romans 8:20-21.
35   Genesis 3:19.
36   John Piper, Sermon, Bethlehem Baptist Church, Minneapolis, MN.
37   Leviticus 26:28, Ezekiel 30:15.
38   Jeremiah 21:13-14.

three

2 RIGHTEOUS VERDICTS

God Rains Down Justice

"A destruction is determined, overflowing with righteousness."[1]
Isaiah, God's Prophet

The apostle tells us that God's wrath is being "revealed from heaven against all ungodliness and unrighteousness."[2] This is present tense. It's happening now, this moment. It's the relentless outworking of God's holiness against the rebellion of mankind. Google tells me 150,000 plus people will die today. It's the "wages of sin."[3] We've all earned our wages. God created man to live. We knowingly chose death. We did that. And death is coming for each of us . . . very, very soon.

False teachers tell us that God will not judge mankind because He is constrained by His love. Well, the false teachers are refuted 150,000 plus times per day. God has judged. God is judging. And God will judge. This is not some isolated, obscure biblical truth. It is in fact, a pervasive scriptural reality. Yes, God is love but obviously, as God, His emotional life is infinitely complex. He is more than one thing. Just as you and I are. "God is love"[4] but He is also "fierce wrath."[5] If we are to have any intellectual integrity with His Word we must affirm that all of God does all that God does—namely, God's justice is expressed in perfect symmetry with His mercy. His compassion is expressed in perfect symmetry with His vengeance. And His wrath is expressed in perfect symmetry with His love. To borrow from John Piper, "There is a perfect beauty and coherence in how all His attributes cooperate. But neither is He without complexity. His character is more like a symphony than a solo performance."[6] Yes, God is love, but He is very much more, as the Bible clearly reveals.

In Peter's second letter, he reveals the sure judgment that will befall every false teacher, and reminds us of Jehovah's unfailing track record in judging His defiant creatures. The apostle tells us that God did not spare the angels who sinned, nor the ancient world of Noah, nor the cities of Sodom and Gomorrah.[7] In the balance of this chapter we will take a closer look at the latter two instances—God's righteous verdicts resulting in both the flood and the destruction of Sodom and Gomorrah.

All But 8

"I will blot out man whom I have created from the face of the land. . . . "[8]

God

You may think you're too sophisticated to believe the biblical account about Noah, the ark, the animals, and the flood . . . but Jesus Christ believed it. As Messiah talked about His second coming and the judgment that would accompany Him, He commented on mankind's unhealthy preoccupation with the immediate and mundane. Then He said:

> For the coming of the Son of Man will be just like the days of Noah. For as in those days which were before the flood they were eating and drinking, they were marrying and giving in marriage, until the day that Noah entered the ark, and they did not understand until the flood came and took them away, so shall the coming of the Son of Man be.[9]

God incarnate had firsthand knowledge of Noah, the ark, the animals, and the flood. He rendered that judgment. He decreed the torrent. He saw to it. If His testimony is not enough for you, I'm not at all sure why you're reading this book. If you're not interested in this God-ordained, biblically revealed, geologically obvious event, initiated and ultimately corroborated by the most credible Witness to ever walk the planet, you might want to put this volume aside and get started on some fiction.

Why?

So, why? Why this global cataclysm? To parrot the last chapter. Sin.

Moses writes:

> Then the LORD saw that the wickedness of man was great on the earth, and that every intent of the thoughts of his heart was only evil continually. And the LORD was sorry that He had made man on the earth, and He was grieved in His heart. And the LORD said. . . . "I, even I am bringing the flood of water upon the earth, to destroy all flesh in which is the breath of life, from under heaven; everything that is on the earth shall perish."[10]

God would save only eight human beings—Noah and his immediate family. Why Noah? Because Noah found favor (or "grace" as the NKJV renders it) in the eyes of the LORD . . . he was a righteous man who walked with God.[11] This is always the biblical pattern. It is the sovereign and initiating grace of God being worked out in the life of a sinner through whom God works His purposes. And the text tells us that "Noah did according to all that the LORD had commanded him"[12] regarding the preparation of the ark. In keeping with His gracious nature, God gave mankind ample warning of the impending doom; for Noah was preaching during the 120 years the ark was under construction.[13] But here is the unvarnished truth about man—not one soul responded. Zero. Nada. Not one would answer the call of God to repent...confirming that God was infallibly just in His verdict of wholesale destruction.

A Deluge of Justice

And the text says that

> In the six hundredth year of Noah's life, in the second month, on the seventeenth day of the month, on the same day all the fountains of the great deep burst open, and the floodgates of the sky opened. And rain fell upon the earth for forty days and forty nights. . . . And the water prevailed more and more upon the earth, so that all the high mountains everywhere under the heavens were covered. . . . Thus He blotted out every living thing that was upon the land, from man to animals to creeping things and to birds of the sky. . . . And the water prevailed upon the earth one hundred and fifty days.[14]

Did you notice the specificity regarding the date the flood began? Yeah, this is not a "once upon a time" thing. This is a historical account; not a fairytale. It is interesting to note that there are more than 300 flood legends throughout the world among widely dispersed people groups. This was a worldwide phenomenon, for "all the high mountains everywhere under the heavens were covered." You can't legitimately hide from that scriptural assertion unless, of course, you're a brazen, out-of-the-closet biblical reductionist—one who enthusiastically edits the Bible with unqualified abandon. You know who you are.

As we are all sadly aware, many so-called Christians don't "kick-in" with the Bible until after Genesis 11, or even later. Yeah, the Garden of Eden, Adam and Eve, Noah's ark, and the Tower of Babel are all just so—what's the word—"unsophisticated"; "unenlightened." The Genesis skeptics believe that anyone with an IQ of 85 or more simply could not condescend to embrace such obvious "folklore." Of course, and again, we're either Bible believers or we're not. The true Christian doesn't stand in judgment over God's Word. We don't presume to have the right to pick and choose what to believe and what to discard or mythologize. The true lover of God is never His editor. Surely, if God can't be trusted to get the first eleven chapters of the Bible right, why would any rational person believe the remaining 1,178 chapters?

The Body Count

Apart from Noah and his family and the creatures in the ark, Genesis tells us that, in this judicial act, God killed every man, woman, boy, and girl, as well as "all flesh in which is the breath of life." How many people were there on the planet? What was the body count? Scholarly estimates run anywhere from 250,000 to 1,000,000,000 plus. No one knows, and ultimately, it's an academic question. Again, God gives life and God takes life. He is the Creator. This is His prerogative. There is an important lesson here for us. God does not put the life of man above His glory. When once His longsuffering patience has been exhausted, He will be glorified in executing perfect justice. He will show forth His righteous indignation. This, of course, is shocking to the nominally Christian and biblically illiterate person—but this is the dangerous God who is.

We do need to stop and think deeply about this. God killed them all. He killed all of them. This is perfect holiness provoked by premeditated, obstinate rebellion. Oh, I hear you. Your god would never do that? Probably not. But as noted earlier, your god is not god. He is a pretender. A cartoon. Your god will do you no good on the day you meet the God who is—the God who "blotted out every living thing upon the face of the land" in a torrential outpouring of divine justice!

A Good Judge

Just what is the job of a good judge? What is he or she supposed to do? Dispense justice. That is the core job description of every judge. Only one thing—dispense justice. It's what God did in the flood. Some might object. But God is on record. He has clearly said that to sin is to die. And again, He alone decides when our wages are due. Yes, God killed 250,000 to 1,000,000,000 + people in the flood. Does that offend you? Why? The wages of sin is death. Holy God says this is justice. Again, you want to protest? Not a good idea to get into that debate with Holy-Other. If that is your chosen course, you will not prevail. In fact, in your self-righteousness and determined arrogance before God, you will only continue to "store up wrath."[15]

We must always remember: God is under no obligation to save anyone. He made everything under the sun. It's His intellectual property. He is the Potter; He can do whatever He wants with "the thing molded,"[16] particularly when His creatures are in abject rebellion against His reign and benevolence. We have no claim on God's forbearance and mercy. All we could possibly claim before God is justice, and we don't want that for we would all land in hell. You and I need grace—the unmerited favor of a justly incensed Sovereign. Remember, too, that God never offered the angels a savior. He simply gave them what their rebellion warranted—justice. He rendered a righteous verdict of condemnation. It's what a good judge should do. It's what He should do with you and me . . . simply dispense justice. So, don't play the fool. Don't critique God for the flood. It was divine justice. Period.

Not Even 10

"Then the LORD *rained on Sodom and Gomorrah brimstone and fire. . . ."*[7]
Moses, God's Prophet

Moses writes, "Now the LORD appeared to [Abraham] by the oaks of Mamre."[18] God had come with good news. There would be a miracle child born to this old man and his barren wife. You know the story. Sarah laughed at the prospect. And God asked, "Is anything too difficult for the LORD?"[19] I know, that verse doesn't really advance the overall thesis of this book, chapter, or section. I just happen to love it. (And well, this is my book after all, so, there it is—one of my favorite verses: just because I can!) It is part of the wonder of biblical Christianity. No one can frustrate our God or turn back His outstretched arm.[20] It is a relentless biblical refrain—our God does whatever He pleases in heaven and earth![21] From miracle babies, to fire and brimstone from heaven.

A Noteworthy Question
The LORD confided in His chosen patriarch regarding the exceedingly grave sin of Sodom and Gomorrah. And Abraham asked,

"Will You indeed sweep away the righteous with the wicked?"[22] This is a noteworthy question. God hasn't mentioned anything about sweeping anyone away. Where does Abraham come up with such a notion? He was only ten generations removed from Noah. Everyone knew what the flood had been about—presumptuous rebellion and provoked Holiness. Abraham didn't formally have Romans 6:23 in his theological lexicon but he didn't need it. He knew what was going on in the cities of the valley. He knew God. He could do the math. He knew what this divine visit meant—wrath, vengeance, recompense, and terror!

The text tells us that Abraham inquired of God regarding the righteous who might be in Sodom. He asked, what if there are 50 righteous there? What about 45 righteous? What about 40? 30? 20? What about 10? And God said, "I will not destroy it on account of the ten . . . and the LORD departed."[23] It's the obvious reason the two angels accompanied the LORD on his visit to Abraham[24] They would continue to Sodom. They were going in to get the righteous.

God's Forcible Rescue

The angels came to Lot, Abraham's nephew who lived in Sodom. Lot recognized them as messengers from God and offered them sanctuary in his home for he knew the dangers of the city. The Genesis text reads that

> . . .the men of Sodom, surrounded the house, both young and old, all the people from every quarter; and they called to Lot . . . "Where are the men who came to you tonight? Bring them out to us that we may have relations with them."[25]

Or, as the Living Bible paraphrase renders it, so that the men of the city could "rape them." Being wholly consumed with homosexual lust, the men of Sodom persisted. So, the angels struck their attackers with blindness to render them harmless. God's emissaries told Lot that the LORD would destroy Sodom. Lot's sons-in-law were not convinced and even Lot himself hesitated. Moses writes:

> So the men seized [Lot's] hand, and the hand of his wife
> and the hands of his daughters, for the compassion of
> the LORD was upon him; and they brought him out and
> put him outside the city.[26]

What a beautiful picture of the attentive and proactive care of God. Despite Lot and his family's hesitation, God's angels "seized" them and brought them out of harm's way. In spite of ourselves, God ensures that His "ministering spirits [are] sent out to render service for the sake of those who will inherit salvation."[27] God is not above forcibly saving His people from their own stupidity. Yes, praise God!

A Modest Salvo

And Genesis tells us that God

> rained on Sodom and Gomorrah brimstone and fire from
> the LORD out of heaven and He overthrew those cities,
> and all the valley, and all the inhabitants of the cities,
> and what grew on the ground . . . and behold, the smoke
> of the land ascended like the smoke of a furnace.[28]

How many died? Obviously, no one knows but God Himself. But we could safely estimate thousands to tens of thousands in the various cities of the "valley." What will be the final body count of God's spent justice as He brings human history on this condemned planet to a close? Ultimately . . . it will be billions. The judgments of the flood, and Sodom and Gomorrah, are but a modest salvo in God's shock-and-awe assault on those who hate Him. This one thing never changes—the wages of sin[29] is always, always, always . . . well, you know.

Only Four Saved

Concerning this Genesis 19 destruction, many have sought to concoct some kind of "natural cause lightning-earthquake-meteor-underground volcano-natural-gas narrative" to explain the valley's destruction. Regarding the source of the fire and brimstone, I prefer to simply quote God's prophet:

And the Ancient of Days took His seat; His vesture was like white snow, and the hair of His head like pure wool. His throne was ablaze with flames, its wheels were a burning fire. A river of fire was flowing and coming out before Him. . . . [30]

It's what the Genesis text tells us. The brimstone and fire rained down from heaven—that holy flow from the very throne of God that Daniel describes. Only four were saved from the fire of heaven. Lot, his wife, and their two daughters. Every other man, woman, boy, and girl in the valley was killed. Even Lot's wife ultimately perished as she longingly looked back to Sodom during the conflagration. Jesus used her death as a warning to those who would set their hearts upon a world under the just condemnation of an incensed God. Christ said, "Remember Lot's wife. Whoever seeks to keep his life shall lose it, and whoever loses his life shall preserve it." [31]

What Jesus Just Kept Saying

As a brief aside, the foregoing saying of Jesus appears no fewer than six times in the Gospels! Although somewhat cryptic, Messiah is saying something huge that He means for us to understand. While I'm pretty sure there are at least twenty sermons here, allow me to simply relay Eugene Peterson's paraphrase of the Lord's words from a couple of the pertinent Gospel texts, and make a quick comment or two. Peterson rephrases the words of Jesus as follows:

If your first concern is to look after yourself, you'll never find yourself. But if you forget about yourself and look to Me, you'll find both yourself and Me. . . . If you grasp and cling to life on your terms, you'll lose it, but if you let that life go, you'll get life on God's terms . . . anyone who holds on to life just as it is destroys that life. But if you let it go . . . you'll have it forever, real and eternal. [32]

If you're wholly vested in this world . . . if your first love is your life here . . . you will lose it all very, very soon. Death is coming for you. The clear inference is—if that is who you are, you have never really lived, and you never will. Jesus is saying, "If you've repented of loving this world and your sin more than Me. . . . If you've stopped loving the life you had without Me and you've begun to love the life you have with Me, then you have found the purpose for which you were created. Indeed, you have started to live, and you will never stop, starting to live!" Yes, that's how everlastingly vast life in Christ is! In Him, we discover that the life we thought we had without Him wasn't life at all. It was a superficial, cartoonish, atrophied counterfeit—a lot of inhaling and exhaling, but no authentic living!

Ultimately, the Lord is saying you must let go of death to seize life. And, oh, by the way, He says, "I am the life."[33] There is a death to be had before you can ever really learn to live. How did the apostle say it? "I have been crucified with Christ; and it is no longer I who live, but Christ lives in me; and the life which I now live in the flesh I live by faith in the Son of God. . . ."[34] Christianity has always been about a crucifixion and a resurrection—not just His, but yours and mine. It's always been about dying to death! As Jesus said many different times, in many different ways, this is, in the end, about the supreme affection of our hearts. Lot's wife loved this world. She refused to die to death, and she perished.

What Compassion Demands

In recounting the biblical narrative of Sodom and Gomorrah, just a word of caution to the contemporary culture. In our postmodern era, where so-called truth is often defined and believed based solely upon self-referential, subjective feelings, many seek to explain away the well-defined teaching of the Bible regarding homosexuality. Such is an impossible task lest you be unconcerned with the distinct meaning of words and any appearance of intellectual integrity. God is unambiguous in both the Old and New Testaments. The Creator is faithful to warn humanity about all sexual sin, including homosexuality. It's like everything else in the cosmos. He invented sex, and it is His sole prerogative to set boundaries upon it. God is explicit. He says that homosexuality is, "an abomination, a detestable act, a degrading passion, unnatural, an indecent act, and gross immorality."[35] There's really no way to spin that.

God says that impenitent sinners, including homosexuals, will not inherit the kingdom of God.[36] It should be noted that the sexual revolution of the last few generations has, as a whole, been extraordinarily effective in overturning fundamental cultural norms that have been in place for millennia. This lamentable fact warrants a strong, clear, repeated, and loving declaration of biblical truth regarding human sexuality where the battle for souls continues to rage. If we are to believe the biblical God, lives and eternities are at stake here—compassion demands that God's truth be spoken concerning all sexual sin.

The Antithesis of Hate Speech

In a blatant assault on the veracity, authority, consistency, and trustworthiness of the Bible as a whole, some claim that Jesus never spoke against homosexuality. This is naked sophistry or just willful ignorance of God and His Self-revelation. The Old Testament God who gave His law through Moses *is* the New Testament incarnate God in that manger. He is the mysterious Trinitarian-God. He is Father, Son, and Spirit. Jesus was unequivocal, stating that "before Abraham was born, I am."[37] He *is* the God who gave Moses the Law and established non-negotiable sexual confines for mankind. Jesus said that He had not come to abolish the Law but to fulfill it.[38] While the New Testament does indeed reveal a "new covenant,"[39] it never sets aside the moral law as originally given. God's Word is crystal clear. Jesus Christ is the God of the Bible—He is not silent on homosexuality. To suggest otherwise can be characterized as nothing less than an exegetical mugging.

Shamelessly, some go further still—actually calling God's Word "hate-speech." Is it not self-evidently true that the hubris of dogged moral revolutionaries today absolutely knows no bounds! But . . . for all who think consistently and are willing to recognize a cosmos governed by absolute truth, the fate of Sodom and Gomorrah alone reveals the fallacy of the "hate speech" attack on the Bible. Truly, God's Word is the antithesis of hate speech. It has always been the exact opposite . . . to the extreme.

God's truth is always love, and to withhold it is always hate. Indeed, in our times when it appears certain that God's Romans 1 judicial abandonment[40] of Western culture is in effect, biblical truth is a most courageous form of love speech. Its why true believers must not be intimidated by the "truth suppressing"[41] speech police. We are called to love people enough to speak His truth. As mature, biblically informed Christians, we don't offer our own small opinions; we simply share God's sovereign proclamations. This is never easy. It's not supposed to be. Jesus told us that just as the world hated Him, it would hate us as well.[42] This reality is no surprise to any who conscientiously walk with the biblical Christ. By His life and death, He taught us the cost of speaking truth. He vividly demonstrated, for the whole world to see and never forget, how very expensive real love can be.

There is Freedom
Parenthetically, for those who have "ears to hear," there is freedom from any and all sexual sin through Jesus Christ—serial fornication, pornography, adultery, homosexuality, etc., etc., etc. There are many testimonies online highlighting the rescuing power of God. If you want deliverance, you can have it. It happens to normal people just like you every day. You are not defined by your sexual desires—you are immeasurably more. And yes, Jesus Christ is way better than the best sex you've ever had! There is liberation if you desire it. It's up to you. God says emancipation is available for any and all sinners. As alluded to earlier, God's apostle writes:

> Do you not know that the unrighteous shall not inherit the kingdom of God? Do not be deceived; neither fornicators, nor idolaters, nor adulterers, nor effeminate, nor homosexuals, nor thieves, nor the covetous, nor drunkards, nor revilers, nor swindlers, shall inherit the kingdom of God. And such were some of you; but you were washed, but you were sanctified, but you were justified in the name of the Lord Jesus Christ, and in the Spirit of God.[43]

"And such were some of you!" The unavoidable deduction being—we're not anymore! God is talking about the deliverance of His people from the oppressive and ultimately lethal slavemaster called sin. You're right, it's what Jesus just kept saying in the Gospels: "Whoever seeks to keep his life shall lose it, and whoever loses his life shall preserve it."[44] Again, to borrow from Peterson, "anyone who holds on to life just as it is destroys that life." Yes, we all must die to death. Close parenthesis.

But Woe to Those Who . . .

Christians understand their very simple role in the world—to merely be the mouthpiece of God in this alien place and to love those around us enough to speak truth. To that end, the prophet and apostle faithfully warn all who would slander and attack God's biblical revelation and His moral constraints. Together they tell us,

> Woe to those who call evil good, and good evil; who substitute darkness for light and light for darkness. . . . Woe to those who are wise in their own eyes, and clever in their own sight . . . [who] give hearty approval to those who practice [sin]."[45]

Woe indeed, for wrath, vengeance, recompense, and terror have been divinely sanctioned and inescapably decreed for each and every rebel who arrogantly flout the sexual and moral restraints established by their Creator!

ℒ

"Hear, O earth: behold, I am bringing disaster. . . ."[46]
God

NOTES

1   Isaiah 10:22.
2   Romans 1:18.
3   Romans 6:23.
4   1 John 4:8.
5   Revelation 19:15.
6   John Piper, *Coronavirus and Christ* (Wheaton, IL: Crossway, 2020), 39.
7   2 Peter 2:4-6.
8   Genesis 6:7.
9   Matthew 24:37-39.
10   Genesis 6:5-6, 17.
11   Genesis 6:8-9.
12   Genesis 7:5.
13   Genesis 6:3, 2 Peter 2:5.
14   Genesis 7:11-24 (excerpts).
15   Romans 2:5.
16   Romans 9:20.
17   Genesis 19:24.
18   Genesis 18:1.
19   Genesis 18:14.
20   Isaiah 14:27.
21   Psalm 135:6.
22   Genesis 18:23.
23   Genesis 18:32-33.
24   Genesis 18:2, Genesis 19:1.
25   Genesis 19:4-5.
26   Genesis 19:16.
27   Hebrews 1:14.
28   Genesis 19:24-25, 28.
29   Romans 6:23.
30   Daniel 7:9-10.
31   Luke 17:32-33.
32   Matthew 10:39, Luke 17:33, John 12:25 (The Message Bible).
33   John 14:6.
34   Galatians 2:20.
35   Leviticus 18:22, 20:13, Romans 1:26-27, Jude 7.
36   I Corinthians 6:9-10.
37   John 8:58.
38   Matthew 5:17.
39   Hebrews 8:13.
40   Romans 1:18-32.
41   Romans 1:18.
42   John 15:18-19.
43   1 Corinthians 6:9-11.
44   Luke 17:32-33.
45   Isaiah 5:20-21, Romans 1:32.
46   Jeremiah 6:19.

four

O First-Born Spared

God in Their Midst

"I will set My eyes against them for evil..."[1]
God

If a farmer plants corn in the spring, he doesn't have to wonder what he will be harvesting come summer. So, too, in the spiritual realm. Job says, "According to what I have seen, those who plow iniquity and those who sow trouble harvest it."[2] God's apostle says it in a most unforgettable way: "Do not be deceived, God is not mocked; for whatever a man sows, this he will also reap."[3] In the street vernacular, we all understand—what goes around, comes around. This is indispensable wisdom, for, indeed, Yahweh is never mocked. Or, as the Message Bible paraphrases, "No one makes a fool of God."[4] In his self-absorbed arrogance, Pharaoh ordered the murder of every firstborn son of Israel.[5] This would come back to him, his progeny, and his nation in the unrelenting, righteous, and terrible judgment of God.

Pharaoh's murderous edict is how Moses got in that wicker basket floating in the Nile. It's why he ended up being adopted by Pharaoh's daughter. It's how he got his name. It's why he was raised as a prince of Egypt becoming a "man of power in words and deeds."[6] But the Bible tells us that

> By faith Moses, when he had grown up, refused to be
> called the son of Pharaoh's daughter, choosing rather to

endure ill-treatment with the people of God than to enjoy the passing pleasures of sin, considering the reproach
of Christ greater riches than the treasures of Egypt; for
he was looking to the reward.[7]

Yeah, it's the reaping and sowing thing. It's true, as John
MacArthur preaches, "From a worldly perspective, Moses was
sacrificing everything for nothing, but from a spiritual perspective, he was sacrificing nothing for everything."[8] Moses wisely
decided that sowing into eternity made far more sense than
sowing into this temporal life.

Yes, Moses faced the same decision each one of us faces. To
align ourselves with the wealth, power, prestige, comfort, security, pleasure, and luxury of this world, or to align ourselves with
God and His invincible purposes. Each of us must weigh it out.
The question always is—Do you hear gain in going with God? Or,
do you hear loss? Jesus says you must choose Me or the world.
You cannot legitimately love both, for either you "will hate the
one and love the other, or [you] will hold to one and despise the
other."[9] God says it's your call. Where is gain for you? What do
you desire? What do you want? What, or who, do you love pre-
eminently? What are you seeking? Are you sowing into this life,
or the next? Are you sowing death or life? For truly, it is a God-
ordained verity, you will eternally reap whatever you temporally
sow. Stop and think about that for sixty seconds.

Moses Called Out
The book of Exodus tells us that God called Moses to be His instrument in delivering Israel out of Egyptian bondage. Moses
asked God His name. His response was, "I AM WHO I AM."[10] As
noted in Chapter One, the Creator is the eternal-self-existent-
transcendent-Other. Simply, the One who has always been and
always will be. As some preacher somewhere said, "God didn't
say I AM whoever you want Me to be as long as you're sincere
about it!"—a pointed indictment upon much of what is called
the modern Christian church. Pseudo-christs abound. Apostate
denominations will preach any christ, just any old christ, but
never the biblical One. The false church is unwilling to proclaim

the fearsome Lion of Judah, the angry Lamb of Revelation 6 who is coming in great wrath.[11] Stayed tuned for Chapter Eight.

Moses tried to excuse himself from God's call no fewer than five times. Considering he was having a supernatural encounter with the Almighty One,[12] his excuses were pretty lame. Yes, just like your excuses and mine when God calls us out of our comfort zones. Moses was making the same mistake we all tend to make when God calls us to go with Him—he was looking at his own résumé and not God's. The latter, of course, renders the former inconsequential. Earlier in the exchange, God had asked Moses what he had in his hand. It was his staff. Essentially, God was saying, "I'll bring miracles and deliverance through your staff; all you really have to do is show up." It's what God always requires of those who profess to be His—show up, believing! It's always our very best worship and our most effective evangelism!

God's Judicial Prerogative

God tells Moses that He will harden Pharaoh's heart so that he will not let Israel go. God instructs Moses:

> Then you shall say to Pharaoh, "Thus says the LORD, 'Israel is My son, My first-born. So I said to you, "Let My son go, that he may serve Me; but you have refused to let him go. Behold, I will kill your son, your first-born.""[13]

God is not mocked! Whatever a man sows, he will most certainly reap. God is always doing two things in the world. Every day He is doing these two things. He is always saving, and He is always judging. As God delivers Israel, He is judging Egypt. Pharaoh is resting comfortably in his luxurious palace completely unaware that he has already been irrevocably judged by his Creator. Nothing has changed outwardly, but it is all over inwardly. God has given Pharaoh over to the just consequences of his own willful rebellion. He's still walking around, living his "good life," but Pharaoh's sentence has been rendered. He is irreversibly damned. He is irretrievably destined to spend an eternity in hell. Naturally, this judicial prerogative of God gives every thinking person serious pause.

Indeed, the gavel has fallen in the courtroom of God. Pharaoh is guilty. Judgment has been pronounced. God will judicially harden Pharaoh's heart even as Pharaoh continues to harden his heart against God. Surely, as is always biblically true, God is sovereign and man is responsible. You may not like it, but that is quite beside the point. The God who is, rules and reigns and manages His cosmos, as well as the lives of men according to His dictates, not yours or mine. God repeatedly reveals that it is always a dangerous dance to presume upon His patience and forbearance. It's the chilling chorus of Romans 1 as the Holy Spirit recounts the judicial decrees of God in giving mankind over to their lusts, their degrading passions, and their depraved minds.[14] It's all over for Pharaoh. His eternal fate is divinely sealed. Only self-absorbed fools play games with Jehovah.

The Ultimate Theodicy

God says to Pharaoh, "For this very purpose I raised you up, to demonstrate My power in you, and that My name might be proclaimed throughout the whole earth."[15] Egypt's destruction is historical evidence of the glory of God revealed in His infinite fury and power in justly devastating His enemies. As the Psalmist reminds us, "The kings of the earth take their stand and . . . take counsel together against the LORD. . . . [And] He who sits in the heavens laughs . . . and scoffs at them."[16] What God did for Israel in crushing Egypt vividly illustrates the ultimate theodicy as the apostle records in Romans 9:22-23:

> What if God, although willing to demonstrate His wrath and to make His power known, endured with much patience vessels of wrath prepared for destruction? And He did so to make known the riches of His glory upon vessels of mercy, which He prepared beforehand for glory. . . .

As Paul reminds us, "Behold then the kindness and severity of God. . . ."[17] God is not simply willing to demonstrate His wrath and power—He is wholeheartedly committed to doing so. Certainly, I AM exercises much patience. But once that tolerance is exhausted, He will bring destruction upon the vessels of wrath

(Egypt) that He may make known the riches of His glory upon the vessels of mercy (Israel). God says:

> I will lay My hand on Egypt and bring out . . . My people the sons of Israel, from the land of Egypt by great judgments. And the Egyptians shall know that I am the LORD, when I stretch out My hand on Egypt. . . . [18]

It's one thing the saved and the damned have forever in common—neither will ever forget that the LORD is God! As we will see, it is the ultimate lesson God would have mankind take away from His utter demolition of Egypt.

God's Adjudication

In his first two appearances before the Egyptian king, Moses delivered God's message, but Pharaoh's heart was hardened, and he refused to let Israel go.[19] The Exodus text documents God unleashing His wrath, vengeance, recompense, and terror upon Egypt. It came in the form of ten judgments. I'm going to summarize each of these plagues for two reasons—one reveals a sobering truth about God and the other reveals a sobering truth about man. First, this account underscores how competent and thorough God is in His judgments. When provoked to it, He is comprehensive, exacting, and exhaustive in His righteous recompense. He will not be distracted nor dissuaded in crushing His enemies. Secondly, this narrative highlights man's absolute and suicidal bent against his Creator, no matter how blatantly obvious the evidences of God's presence, power, and glory are. We need to learn and never forget that: God was relentless in His wrath upon Egypt as He will be against every person who remains His adversary. And, we need to learn and never forget that: Pharaoh was relentless in his obstinance toward God as are all men who love their sin more than their Creator. Note God's rigor: He painstakingly destroys His enemy. Note Pharaoh's tenacity: he is utterly unyielding in his rebellion against God. Yes, right here, the truth about God and the truth about man played out in ten judgements highlighting God's sovereign power over His creation and His enemies! Behold, the fate of all who refuse to acknowledge that the LORD is God! Moses records the . . .

First plague—In turning the Nile to blood, making it foul (Chapter 7)
- The Egyptian magicians mimicked the act.
- Pharaoh was unconcerned and his "heart was hardened."
- Pharaoh did not yet acknowledge that the LORD is God.

Second plague—Of frogs covering the land, invading every house (Chapter 8)
- The Egyptian magicians mimicked the act.
- Pharaoh feigned repentance, petitioning Moses to ask God for relief.
- God granted relief, but Pharaoh "hardened his heart."
- Pharaoh did not yet acknowledge that the LORD is God.

Third plague—Of lice/gnats (Chapter 8)
- The Egyptian magicians could not mimic this act.
- The magicians told Pharaoh it was the finger of God.
- "But Pharaoh's heart was hardened."
- Pharaoh did not yet acknowledge that the LORD is God.

Fourth plague—Of flies/insects (Chapter 8)
- God set a division between the house of Egypt and the house of Israel so there were no insects in Goshen where the Hebrews resided.
- Pharaoh feigned repentance, petitioning Moses to ask God for relief.
- God granted relief, not one insect remained, but "Pharaoh hardened his heart."
- Pharaoh did not yet acknowledge that the LORD is God.

Fifth plague—Of livestock pestilence (Chapter 9)
- God set a division between the livestock of Egypt and the livestock of Israel so that none of the Hebrews' livestock died.
- All the livestock of Egypt died.
- "But the heart of Pharaoh was hardened."
- Pharaoh did not yet acknowledge that the LORD is God.

Sixth plague—Of boils on man and beast (Chapter 9)
- The boils were through all the land of Egypt.
- And "the LORD hardened Pharaoh's heart."
- Pharaoh did not yet acknowledge that the LORD is God.

Seventh plague—Of hail and flashing fire (Chapter 9)
- This was upon the house of Egypt but not upon the house of Israel in Goshen.
- Pharaoh feigned repentance, petitioning Moses for relief which God granted.
- Pharaoh "sinned again and hardened his heart."
- Pharaoh did not yet acknowledge that the LORD is God.

Eighth plague—Of locusts (Chapter 10)
- God hardened Pharaoh's heart that He might perform His signs, making a mockery of the Egyptians so all may know that He is the LORD.
- Pharaoh's servants told him to let Israel go for "Egypt is destroyed."
- Locusts covered the "whole land so that the land was darkened."
- Pharaoh feigned repentance, petitioning Moses for relief, which God granted.
- "But the LORD hardened Pharaoh's heart" and he did not let Israel go.
- Pharaoh did not yet acknowledge that the LORD is God.

Ninth plague—Of darkness (Chapter 10)
- There was a "darkness that could be felt" over all the land for three days.
- "The sons of Israel had light in their dwellings."
- Pharaoh feigned repentance, petitioning Moses for relief.
- "But the LORD hardened Pharaoh's heart" and he did not let Israel go.
- Pharaoh did not yet acknowledge that the LORD is God.

The Last Plague

How did the apostle say it? "Do not be deceived, God is not mocked; for whatever a man sows, this he will also reap."[20] God's spiritual laws are fixed. God is never made a fool. After multiple warnings from God's servant and nine, up-close-and-personal divine judgements, Pharaoh was recalcitrant. Full of defiant arrogance, he would not acknowledge that the LORD is God. Sure, he had feigned repentance a number of times, but he was only playing a game with God that billions are playing to this day. This is always fatal as is evident from the pages of Scripture. Pharaoh exercised his will and hardened his heart. God exercised His will and hardened Pharaoh's heart. It's a biblical axiom. God allows men to exercise their will, but, most assuredly, He will exercise His.

God told Moses . . .

> About midnight I am going out into the midst of Egypt, and all the first-born in the land of Egypt shall die, from the first-born of Pharaoh who sits on his throne, even to the first-born of the slave girl who is behind the millstone; all the first-born of the cattle as well. [But] Pharaoh will not listen to you, so that My wonders will be multiplied in the land of Egypt. . . . I will execute judgment—I am the LORD.[21]

In effect, God says this is personal. Again, sin always is with God. He says, *I will kill*[22] all the first-born of Egypt. As I have noted earlier and will continue to remind you throughout the book, this is God's divine right. He gives life and He takes life. This is His business. He renders our sin-wages, our recompense, to us as seems good to Him. Our thoughts on the matter could not be more inconsequential. And the text reads, "Now it came about at midnight that the LORD struck all the first-born in the land of Egypt . . . and there was no home where there was not someone dead."[23] Obviously, we don't know how many died. I've seen estimates of 20,000 to 100,000 plus. Again, the numbers are academic. The underlying reality is that the God who is, the biblical God, will execute His perfect justice, in accordance with His unimpeachable purposes and based solely upon His flawless timetable. In this, Yahweh does not consult men nor seek their sanction.

Passed Over

As God judges Egypt, He delivers Israel. In this rescue, God is foreshadowing His ultimate deliverance of His worldwide remnant through Messiah, Jesus Christ. God instructed the Hebrews to take an unblemished male sheep or goat and kill it, putting some of the blood on the doorposts and lintel of the house.[24] And God said, "When I see the blood I will pass over you, and no plague will befall you to destroy you when I strike the land of Egypt."[25] For indeed, as He has promised, God will save a people purchased with the precious blood of Christ from every tribe, and tongue, and people, and nation.[26] This Old Testament imagery of the New Testament reality is impossible to miss or mistake. Jesus Christ is the Lamb that was slain.[27] We are blood-bought sinners, "being justified as a gift by His grace through the redemption which is in Christ Jesus; whom God displayed publicly as a propitiation in His blood through faith. . . . "[28] The "destroyer"[29] will pass over the true believer because of the spilled blood of Jesus Christ. God says though His prophet, ". . .there is no other God besides Me, a righteous God and a Savior; there is none except Me."[30]

That You May Know!

Because an adequate First Cause is rationally necessary, and because there simply are no other intelligible God-revelations in the world apart from the Bible, mankind knows Yahweh is God. In his first exchange with Moses, Pharaoh told him that "I do not know the LORD." While this is obviously true in a relational sense, it is utterly false in a hardwiring sense—that is to say, in the essential and unique way in which God has designed and constructed humanity. Specifically, we do indeed know that the LORD is God. There is no ambiguity in the Bible. It's not that men don't know, it's that they do.

> Because that which is known about God is evident within them; for God made it evident to them. For since the creation of the world His invisible attributes, His eternal power and divine nature have been clearly seen, being understood through what has been made, so that they are without excuse.[31]

While man viscerally and intuitively knows that God is there, when He comes in wrath, mankind must cognitively deal with the dangerous-God reality. God says it several times in the Exodus account—that as He reveals His sovereignty and omnipotent power in judgment, both Egypt and Israel will *know* that He is the LORD.[32] God frequently says this in Scripture. Men are never quite so willing to recognize their Creator than when He comes in holy fury and vengeance. As noted, every human being instinctively knows that the LORD is God, but amid His judgment, each impenitent soul must grudgingly come face to face with this supreme cosmic reality. Indeed, the LORD will compel Pharaoh to concede that He is God! In the utter destruction of his nation, the Egyptian king will ultimately have no choice but to acknowledge that Yahweh is God. Truly, it will be the ever-present realization that will utterly overwhelm and grip his mind for a billion eternities in hell.

Fear and Belief

God says:

> Thus, I will harden Pharaoh's heart, and he will chase af-
> ter [Israel]; and I will be honored through Pharaoh and
> . . . all his army . . . through his chariots and his horsemen
> [and] and the Egyptians will know that I am the LORD.[33]

You know the story. In their exodus, the Hebrews are backed
up against the Red Sea and are in a panic as Pharaoh's chariots
approach. Moses says a beautiful thing that every true believer
knows is true. He says, "The LORD will fight for you."[34] God blasts
a pathway through the sea and Israel passes through to safety.
The whole Egyptian military goes in after them.

> And the waters returned and covered the chariots and
> the horsemen, even Pharaoh's entire army that had
> gone into the sea after [Israel]; not even one of them re-
> mained. . . . And when Israel saw the great power which
> the LORD had used against the Egyptians, the people
> feared the LORD, and they believed in the LORD and in
> His servant Moses.[35]

Terror and Dread

It's just always true. In wrath, vengeance, recompense, and terror,
the awesome, fearsome God of the Bible is terrifyingly magnified
in the eyes of men. God will vanquish His enemies. God will deliver His people. All will know that the LORD is God! You simply
must go read the song Israel sang to the LORD after watching
Him fight for them. Here are just a few excerpts . . .

> The LORD is a warrior. . . . Your right hand, O LORD is
> majestic in power, [it] shatters the enemy. And in the
> greatness of Your excellence You overthrow those who
> rise up against You; You send forth Your burning anger
> and it consumes them as chaff. Who is like You among
> the gods, O LORD? Who is like You, majestic in holiness,
> awesome in praises, working wonders? The peoples have

heard, they tremble; anguish has gripped [them]. . . .
Terror and dread fall upon them; by the greatness of
Your arm they are motionless as stone. . . . The LORD
shall reign forever and ever.[36]

Ultimately, every human being will acknowledge that the
LORD is God. Every knee will bow, and every tongue will confess
that Jesus Christ is Lord to the glory of God the Father.[37] Even the
damned. In experiencing God's wrath poured out against him,
Pharaoh finally believed that the LORD is God. Truly, he will never stop believing it, for there are no unbelievers in hell.

*"You, even You, are to be feared; And who may stand in Your
presence when once You are angry?"*[38]
God's Psalmist

NOTES

1   Amos 9:4.
2   Job 4:8.
3   Galatians 6:7.
4   Galatians 6:7, (The Message Bible).
5   Exodus 1:16, 22.
6   Acts 7:22.
7   Hebrews 11:24-26.
8   John MacArthur, Sermon, Grace Community Church, Los Angeles, CA.
9   Matthew 6:24.
10 Exodus 3:14.
11 Revelation 5:5, 6:16-17.
12 Revelation 4:8.
13 Exodus 4:22-23.
14 Romans 1:24-28.
15 Romans 9:17.
16 Psalm2:2,4.
17 Romans 11:22.
18 Exodus 7:4-5.
19 Exodus 7:13-14.
20 Galatians 6:7.
21 Exodus 11:4-5, 9, 12:12.
22 Exodus 4:22-23.
23 Exodus 12:29-30.
24 Exodus 12:5-7.
25 Exodus 12:13.
26 1 Peter 1:19, Revelation 5:9.
27 Revelation 5:12.
28 Romans 3:24-25.
29 Exodus 12:23.
30 Isaiah 45:21.
31 Romans 1:19-20.
32 Exodus 7:5, 17, 8:22.
33 Exodus 14:4, 17-18.
34 Exodus 14:14.
35 Exodus 14:28, 31.
36 Exodus 15:3-18.
37 Philippians 2:10-11.
38 Psalm 76:7.

five

33 KINGDOMS ANNIHILATED

God's Instrument of Wrath

"The LORD *determined to destroy. . . . "*[1]
Jeremiah, God's Prophet

The Genesis text tells us that in a night of "terror and great darkness"[2] God made a covenant with Abraham.

This is yet another commentary on the holy otherness of God. Terror and darkness in the presence of Yahweh are not infrequent biblical allusions. It is reminiscent of the account at Mount Sinai when God met with Moses. In recounting that meeting, the prophet reveals that

> . . .there were thunder and lightning flashes and a thick cloud and a very loud trumpet sound so that all the people who were in the camp trembled. . . . Mount Sinai was all in smoke because the LORD descended upon it in fire . . . and the mountain quaked violently. . . . Moses spoke and God answered with thunder. . . . And when the people saw it, they trembled. . . . [And] said to Moses "Speak to us yourself . . . but let not God speak to us, lest we die."[3]

The parallel account in the book of Hebrews records that Sinai was

a blazing fire, and . . . darkness and gloom and whirlwind
. . . and the sound of words which sound was such that
those who heard begged that no further word should be
spoken to them. . . . And so terrible was the sight, that
Moses said, I am full of fear and trembling."4

Jehovah is awesome. He is fearsome. He is dreadful. He is
frightening. This is all true because He is holy-other. He pro-
vokes fear, trembling, and terror in the heart of fallen man even
when encountered in His veiled glory. It's the natural confronted
by the Supernatural. As earlier stated, it is the ultimate trauma
for mankind. This is the unanimous and universal testimony of
Scripture. The prophet's words are true—in the holy presence of
God, mankind is instinctively inclined to hide "from the terror
of the LORD and from the splendor of His majesty."5 Yes, I understand your god may not be like this. But you urgently need to
know that if he is not, your god is not God. At best, he's no more
than an Aesop's fable.

Please excuse my brief digression in Exodus and Hebrews. As
you may have already gathered, I dearly love BIG-GOD texts. I
throw them in upon the slightest of provocations. So, back to
God's Genesis 15 covenant with Abraham. The LORD promised
His patriarch a son and descendants as numerous as the stars.
Then God guaranteed Abraham's progeny the land "from the
river of Egypt as far as the great river, the river Euphrates."6 God
foretold of the enslavement of Israel in Egypt for 400 years and
His subsequent judgment of Pharaoh. Then God said something
particularly noteworthy to Abraham concerning His ways in
righteously judging humanity. God told him that the Hebrews
would not return to the land until the fourth generation because
"the iniquity of the Amorites is not yet complete."7

Comprehensive Debauchery

What is God saying about the Amorites (Canaanites) and their
sin? That they are in the midst of a Romans 1 judgment. God has
exercised His judicial privilege. He has given the Amorites over
to their lusts and degrading passions. It's the reprobate mind.
Judgment is set and God's timing will be perfect. God said that

these peoples had engaged in "every abominable act which the LORD hates . . . for they even burn their sons and daughters in the fire to their gods."[8] This is ultimate wickedness personified.

No, this wasn't just a little sin. This was wholesale, complete, and perfect revolution against the God who is and His moral boundaries. They denied themselves no self-indulgence. It was comprehensive debauchery. They practiced every conceivable sexual sin, including incest, adultery, homosexuality, and even bestiality.[9] The inhabitants of Canaan were not cognizant of the fact that their sins were being vigilantly tallied and logged.[10] They didn't know the precise moment when they would commit their last act of rebellion against their Creator . . . that very last deed of willful and haughty arrogance before God . . . that very last sin. But God did. The die was cast. God would deliver Israel at just the right time to, in turn, use them as His vehicle of judgment upon the degenerate peoples of Canaan. Justice for every single, high-handed sin against God had been inviolably decreed and would come to pass. Recompense was coming and would be delivered through the business end of a Jewish sword.

Wonder and Wrath

As God delivers Israel from Egypt in preparation to judge Canaan, there were many wonders and much wrath. Concerning God's work in this regard, Moses writes, "Since the day that God created man on the earth . . . has anything been done like this great thing or has anything been heard like it?"[11] The answer of course is an unqualified no!

He continues:

> Has any people heard the voice of God speaking from the midst of the fire. . . . Or has a god tried to go to take for himself a nation from within another nation by trials, by signs and wonders and by war by a mighty hand and by an outstretched arm and by great terrors as the LORD your God did for you in Egypt before your eyes? To you it was shown that you might know that the LORD, He is God; there is no other besides Him.[12]

Contrary to many who call themselves preachers today, God is not ashamed of His "signs, wonders, war, mighty hand, outstretched arm, and great terrors" that He violently unleashes upon His enemies. In the Bible, El-Shaddai repeatedly and unreservedly calls attention to His vengeance being poured out upon His foes. He continually says that by this—by His spent wrath—men will know that He is the LORD! God means for men to know that He is LORD by, and through, His fury! And yes, without fail, every man will know, either in the receipt of His grace or in the delivery of His anger. So, if your preacher is sheepish in proclaiming the glory of God in His divine severity, you urgently need to find a new preacher.

In the Exodus, as God is leading Israel toward the Promised Land, He tells them that they "shall utterly destroy"[13] the inhabitants of Canaan. The prophet writes that God "repays those who hate Him to their faces, to destroy them. . . . "[14] Concerning the cities of Canaan, God says, "You shall not leave alive anything that breathes."[15] Yes, regarding the wantonly wicked, it is an unqualified biblical verity, "The LORD will swallow them up in His wrath."[16] Israel will be the instrument of God's wrath, vengeance, recompense, and terror in Canaan. Judgment is fixed and appointed. God has set His face against His adversaries.

God's Exodus Instruction

During the Exodus, God taught Israel. He told them that in obedience there would be blessing, abundance, protection, security, victory, peace, provision, and multiplication—not to mention, His promise to "walk among" them.[17]

Furthermore, God warned that, if they did not obey Him, if they rejected His statutes, abhorred His ordinances, and ignored His commandments . . .

I, in turn, will do this to you: I will appoint over you a sudden terror, consumption and fever . . . also, you shall sow your seed uselessly. . . . And I will set My face against you so that you shall be struck down before your enemies. . . . And your land shall not yield its produce. . . . If then you act in hostility against Me . . . then I will act in hostility against you. . . . I will bring a sword upon you which will execute vengeance. . . . I will send a pestilence. . . . Yet if in spite of this, you do not obey Me but act with hostility against Me . . . then I will act with wrathful hostility against you. . . . Further you shall eat the flesh of your sons and the flesh of your daughters you shall eat . . . for My soul shall abhor you. . . . [18]

So, obedience or disobedience? This is not complicated. This is not hard. Am I right? God's blessing or God's vengeance? This is the very simple choice God puts in front of every person. It's always our call—our decision. Unfortunately, as we will see more fully in the next chapter, Israel chose to "act in hostility against" God, repeatedly—the God who had not only revealed Himself to them, but had proven Himself to them over, and over, and over again. It raises the question, doesn't it? Why decide against an Omnipotent-Holy-Benevolent-Wrathful-Sovereign? It's the Genesis 3 question. It's the same question before each of us. Obey or defy? Again, for the thoughtful person, this is not difficult to sort out.

Rebellion Along the Way

Inexplicably, there was trouble on the way to the Promised Land. Israel had seen the jaw-dropping presence and power of God in their deliverance. Yet, they decided that what they really needed to do was worship a golden calf.[19] On the surface, this sequence of events is beyond comprehension. However, it is an unvarnished look into the human heart with its propensity to turn away from God with absolutely no coherent rationale. Yes, we are all broken in the most profound way. We are given to bizarre fits of sheer insanity called sin. The Exodus text tells us that as God's anger burned, so did the anger of Moses. And Moses said, "Whoever is for the LORD, come to me!"[20] The Levites responded, and Moses instructed them to move through the camp killing every man who persisted in rebellion against God. About 3,000 men fell.[21]

Later, as Israel is poised to cross the Jordan, they camped at Shittim. Again, they decided it might be a good idea to play religion with a local idol. The text reads that the LORD was angry against Israel. And the LORD said to Moses, "Take all the leaders of the people and execute them in broad daylight . . . so that the fierce anger of the LORD may turn away from Israel."[22]

In addition to the commanded execution, God sent a plague among the people and 24,000 died.[23] You don't get to play fast and loose with I AM. Ever. You don't get to presume on His forbearance. Ever. You don't get to play religion in apostate denominations with their pseudo-christs. Ever. As we have already seen in our very abbreviated review of Scripture thus far, sometimes God is longsuffering. Sometimes He is not. Premeditated, habitual, lifestyle sin against God, garnished with a little pseudo-Christianity, is like a perpetual game of Russian Roulette. Sooner or later, with sudden finality, you die—forever.

God's Vengeance
And God told Moses, "Be hostile to the Midianites and strike them,"[24] for they had enticed and facilitated Israel's idolatry at Shittim. In the action, the army of Israel killed every Midianite male but spared the women and children. The text reads:

And Moses was angry . . . and said to them "Have you spared all the women? . . . Now therefore kill every male among the little ones, and kill every woman who has known man intimately. But all the girls who have not known man intimately, spare for yourselves. . . . "[25]

I know some who are merely churchgoers are highly offended at such a statement. I mean, what could possibly be the rationale for this? Well, a holy Creator-God provoked is answer enough. God's perfect justice works as a more than compelling answer. Or, the outworking of God's fearsome righteousness fits the circumstance. Again, God does not put the life of man, woman, boy, or girl above His purpose, His law, and His glory. Ultimately, God unapologetically commanded "full vengeance"[26] and used Israel to effect it. You don't have to like it. God doesn't care if you like it or not. He is not seeking your approval or mine. God did it. He is the final arbiter in all matters concerning sin and judgment. That is simply enough said for the born-again lover of God.

True believers never dare critique infinite Mind and His holy acts with our two-and-a-half pounds of fallen, sinful, carnal, temporal, finite gray matter. The genuine Christian is always willing to tremble before God, but never, never, never call Him to account for His actions. This severe judgment on the malignant rebels of Midian was justice for them and mercy for Israel. Specifically, God was purging the base, corrupt, and idolatrous influences of the Midianites from the area for the long-term benefit of His people. Also, God graciously spared the virgin girls that they might be assimilated into the Jewish nation. Remember that whenever you find yourself recoiling at God's ways in judgment, you must never forget two simple things. He is always right. And you, are always wrong.

Justice for 33 Kings
Before God called Moses to Himself in death, Israel took out two kings east of the Jordan. It was utter annihilation. Moses writes:

> So we captured all [King Sihon's] cities . . . and utterly destroyed the men, women and children of every city. We left no survivors. . . . So the LORD our God delivered Og also, king of Bashan, with all his people into our hand, and we smote them until no survivor was left.[27]

Then Israel, led by Joshua, turned its collective eye west, across the Jordan. God would use Joshua to bring judgment to thirty-one kings. In the remainder of the chapter, we'll take an abbreviated look at that conquest-judgement account.

The King of Jericho
You are likely to know the story of how God supernaturally brought down the walls of this fortified city. As noted earlier, all the Hebrews had to do was basically show up. God would do the rest. Joshua writes that Israel, "utterly destroyed everything in the city, both man and woman, young and old, ox and sheep and donkey, with the edge of the sword."[28]

The King of Ai
And God told Joshua, "And you shall do to Ai and its king just as you did to Jericho. . . . "[29] Israel attacked, Joshua writes, "And all who fell that day both men and women, were 12,000—all the people of Ai."[30] All the inhabitants of Ai were "utterly destroyed."[31]

The Amorite Kings
This conquest of the Amorite coalition is found in Joshua 10. Following are some paraphrased and condensed excerpts:

> Verse 10—The LORD confounded the Amorites and slew them with a great slaughter.
> Verse 11—The LORD threw large hail stones from heaven and they died.
> Verse 20—And Israel slayed them with a very great slaughter.
> Verse 26—And Joshua put the Amorite kings to death.
> Verse 28—The city of Makkedah was utterly destroyed and every person in it.
> Verse 30—The city of Libnah was struck with the edge of the sword. No survivors.
> Verse 32—Every person in the city of Lachish was struck by the edge of the sword.
> Verse 33—Horam, King of Gezer, came against Israel. There were no survivors.
> Verse 35—Every person in the city of Eglon was struck with the edge of the sword.
> Verse 37—There were no survivors in the city of Hebron.
> Verse 39—The city of Debir was utterly destroyed. There were no survivors.

Regarding this region of Canaan, the text tells us that Joshua

> struck all the land. . . . He left no survivor, but he utterly destroyed all who breathed, just as the LORD, the God of Israel, had commanded. And Joshua struck them . . . [and] captured all these kings and their lands at one time, because the LORD, the God of Israel, fought for Israel.[32]

The Kings of Northern Canaan

The Northern kings came out to fight Israel. God told Joshua, "Do not be afraid . . . for tomorrow . . . I will deliver all of them slain before Israel. . . . And the LORD delivered them into the hand of Israel, so . . . no survivor was left. . . ."[33] Then Joshua captured all the cities of the northern kings "and struck every person . . . with the edge of the sword, utterly destroying them; there was no one left who breathed."[34]

God's judgment of the peoples of Canaan was complete. In obstinately practicing their lifestyles of gross sin, they had willfully hardened their hearts against their Creator. And in their judgment, "it was of the LORD to harden their hearts, to meet Israel in battle in order that He might utterly destroy them, that they might receive no mercy, but that He might destroy them."[35] It's one of the indisputable lessons of the Bible—when once God is aroused to destruction, He is proficient.

God's Faithfulness and Joshua's Warning

The biblical God never doesn't keep a promise. This is true whether He's talking about blessing or curse. As previously noted, He is utterly faithful in each circumstance. Not one promise of blessing, and not one promise of judgment will fail—each and every one of them will come to pass in God's impeccable timing. The sun may or may not come up tomorrow, but the Creator-God could not be more clear, "My word . . . which goes forth from My mouth...shall not return to Me empty, without accomplishing what I desire. . . ."[36] For indeed, the biblical God "does according to His will in the host of heaven and among the inhabitants of the earth; And no one can ward off His hand. . . ."[37]

Regarding God's faithfulness concerning the Promised Land, Joshua writes:

> So the LORD gave Israel all the land which He had sworn to give to their fathers, and they possessed it and lived in it. . . . Not one of the good promises which the LORD had made to the house of Israel failed; all came to pass.[38]

Concerning God's faithfulness in judgment, Joshua, speaking prophetically, told Israel that they would

> . . .not be able to serve the LORD, for He is a holy God. He is a jealous God; He will not forgive your transgression or your sins. If you forsake the LORD and serve foreign gods, then He will turn and do you harm and consume you after He has done good to you.[39]

We will see God's faithfulness concerning these promises in the next chapter.

Don't Call Yourself a Christian if You're This Guy

Regarding the first six books of the Bible, I once heard a dignified church member say something to the effect that his god "would never command the killing of women and children." I suspect there are millions of people who profess to be Christians who would heartily concur with such a sentiment. Once again, we're either Bible believers or we're not. But if you're this guy, I would caution you in the strongest possible terms that you are worshipping an emasculated, counterfeit, sub-biblical, pseudo-god. Your god is not God. He is not the God of the Bible. He is not the dangerous God who is. And yes, you will very soon learn, firsthand, that God is meticulously faithful regarding His "threatenings."[40] If you don't bow to the "terrifyingly magnificent"[41] God of the Bible—the One who kills men, women, boys, and girls in accordance with His righteous judgements—wrath, vengeance, recompense, and terror will soon be yours.

☙

"Your ways and your deeds have brought these things to you.
This is your evil. . . . "[42]
Jeremiah, God's Prophet

NOTES

1 Lamentations 2:8.
2 Genesis 15:12.
3 Exodus 19:16, 18-19, 20:18-19.
4 Hebrews 12:18-19, 21.
5 Isaiah 2:10.
6 Genesis 15:18.
7 Genesis 15:16.
8 Deuteronomy 12:31.
9 See Leviticus 18:3-27.
10 Revelation 20:12-13.
11 Deuteronomy 4:32.
12 Deuteronomy 4:33-35.
13 Deuteronomy 7:2.
14 Deuteronomy 7:10.
15 Deuteronomy 20:16.
16 Psalm 21:9.
17 Leviticus 26:1-12.
18 Leviticus 26:16-30 (excerpts).
19 Exodus 32:1-4.
20 Exodus 32:26.
21 Exodus 32:27-28.
22 Numbers 25:3-4.
23 Numbers 25:9.
24 Numbers 25:17.
25 Numbers 31:14-15,17-18.
26 Numbers 31:2.
27 Deuteronomy 2:34, 3:3.
28 Joshua 6:21.
29 Joshua 8:2.
30 Joshua 8:25.
31 Joshua 8:26.
32 Joshua 10:40-42.
33 Joshua 11:6, 8.
34 Joshua 11:11.
35 Joshua 11:20.
36 Isaiah 55:11.
37 Daniel 4:35.
38 Joshua 21:43, 45.
39 Joshua 24:19-20.
40 A. W. Pink, *The Attributes of God* (Grand Rapids MI: Baker Book House, 1995), 54.
41 John Piper, *Spectacular Sins* (Wheaton, IL: Crossway, 2008), 13.
42 Jeremiah 4:18.

SIX

12 PROPHETS PROCLAIM FURY

God's Promised Consequence

". . .I shall bring all your abominations upon you. . . .
Your doom has come to you."[1]
God

God hates mere religion. He always has.

Jesus Christ didn't mince His words. He pronounced damnation upon the religious leaders of His day, saying:

> Woe, woe, woe to you . . . for you are like whitewashed
> tombs . . . even so you too outwardly appear righteous to
> men, but inwardly you are full of hypocrisy and lawlessness . . . how shall you escape the sentence of hell?[2]

Religion is Satan's best con. He's the "father of lies".[3] And his religious fictions are taking billions to hell. It's the ultimate demonic scam. This, of course, includes the many and varied forms of pseudo-Christianity with its caricatured-christs—no doubt, the adversary's proudest achievement! Affinity for me-centered religion is a pristine reflection of mankind's depraved heart. Man has always preferred a self-righteous, user-friendly, feel-good formula that can be employed to manage a custom-made deity. Domesticated gods are just so much more expedient. Denominational banality and rote ecclesiastical performance are simply a lot less bothersome than true repentance and unconditional obedience—the explicit call of the Son of God to anyone who would claim Him as Lord and Savior.

Pleasant Words, Illusions, Ear-Tickles, and Myths
This fondness to leave the revealed truth and power of the biblical God for a low-stress, comfortable religious habit is graphically depicted in both Testaments. Apostasy inevitably metastasizes in the clergy—unprincipled, duplicitous, self-serving, cowardly, professional, so-called ministers who are quite content to give the people exactly what they desire. There are numerous places to authenticate this reality in the Old Testament. Isaiah says it as well as any:

> For this is a rebellious people, false sons, sons who refuse to listen to the instruction of the LORD; Who say . . . to the prophets, "You must not prophesy to us what is right, speak to us pleasant words, prophesy illusions."[4]

The apostle warned of the same heretical drift in the New Testament—something that is clearly a full-blown epidemic in what is called the church today. Paul writes:

> For the time will come when they will not endure sound doctrine; but wanting to have their ears tickled, they will accumulate for themselves teachers in accordance to their own desires; and will turn away their ears from the truth, and will turn aside to myths.[5]

Pleasant words, illusions, unsound doctrine, and ear-tickling-teachers propagating myths—sounds like your average so-called Christian church almost anywhere in the world right now. Obviously, this is a can't-miss-church-growth strategy! A lot of people like church just fine as long as an emasculated god is served up. Old Testament Israel preferred an edited god and employed their prophets for hire to lead the way. Jeremiah gives us God's assessment of these leaders and the calamitous consequences for the Jewish nation:

The prophets prophesy falsely, and the priests rule on their own authority; And My people love it so! . . . Behold, the word of the LORD has become a reproach to them; They have no delight in it. . . . They refused to take correction. . . . They have refused to repent. . . . Their transgressions are many, their apostasies are numerous . . . . "Shall I not punish these people," declares the LORD, "And on a nation such as this shall I not avenge Myself?...Do you not fear Me?" declares the LORD. "Do you not tremble in My presence?...I will stretch out My hand against the inhabitants of the land..."[6]

This Chapter's Goal

In this chapter, we'll just let God speak with a minimum of commentary. When you read His graphic words of judgment given through His prophets, you will understand. My goal is to simply summarize in abbreviated fashion God's pronouncements of condemnation upon Judah, Israel, and surrounding nations through twelve of His writing prophets. I will endeavor to succinctly capture the essence of each prophet's message as it relates to God's edict against those in rebellion against Him. Ultimately, this is God's word of judgment to any and all who would arrogantly disregard Him—particularly those who are guilty of feigning allegiance to Him. God is not unclear about mere religious performance—He loathes it! The Old Testament prophets leave no doubt concerning those who are, at heart, indifferent toward Yahweh—yes, there will be much wrath, vengeance, recompense, and terror. This is an indispensable lesson for every one of us to hear, understand, and take to heart. The dangerous God who is, does not tolerate spiritual infidelity—He crushes it!

A Wake-Up Call

I entreat you not to read the following excerpts at your normal pace. It will be immensely profitable for you to linger over the selected words, phrases, and verses—to fully take each one into your heart and mind . . . to feel the weight of them. In thoughtfully considering the awful vengeance of God in the physical realm, you will, in turn, get a small sense of how monstrous your sin is in the spiritual realm. In His many and varied judgments, God is telling us something about ourselves and our moral rebellion. God's spent wrath is, to borrow from John Piper again, a "wake-up call, telling us that sin leads to things like this!"[7] God means for us to awaken from our "dreamworld of thinking our sin is no big deal. It's a horrifically big deal."[8] If prayerfully considered, God might very well use His words on the next few pages to dramatically alter the rest of your life . . . and beyond!

Obadiah

God condemns Israel's nemesis Edom for its arrogance while alluding to the final and ultimate judgment of all nations. God says:

> I will bring you down . . . by slaughter . . . and you will be cut off forever. . . . For the day of the LORD draws near on all the nations. As you have done, it will be done to you. Your dealings will return on your head . . . there will be no survivor of the house of [Edom].[9]

Joel

The prophet preached during a severe drought and locust invasion. He used those calamities to prefigure the judgment of God. To give you a sense of the book—following are some select words, a phrase, and one verse in its entirety. Joel writes:

> Wail, mourn, ruined, destroyed, lament, destruction, desolate, tremble, thick darkness, gloom, consuming fire, anguish, all faces turn pale. . . . The day of the LORD is indeed great and very awesome, and who can endure it?[10]

Hosea

Hosea reveals that in God's judicial response to wanton sin, He withdraws from those who have abandoned themselves to unrestrained depravity. God gives such rebels over to their debased desires. Regarding Israel, the prophet writes:

Their deeds will not allow them to return to their God. For a spirit of harlotry is within them. They will . . . seek the LORD, but they will not find Him; He has withdrawn from them. They have dealt treacherously against the LORD. . . . "Woe to them, for they have strayed from Me! Destruction is theirs, for they have rebelled against Me! They have gone deep in depravity. . . . Therefore, a tumult will arise among your people. . . . Samaria will be held guilty, for she has rebelled against her God. They will fall by the sword, their little ones will be dashed to pieces, and their pregnant women will be ripped open."[11]

Amos

In a time of peace and prosperity, the prophet addressed the utter loss of true worship in a culture that had become altogether corrupt. Amos writes:

If a calamity occurs in a city has not the LORD done it. . . . A lion has roared! Who will not fear?... "And in all the vineyards there is wailing, because I shall pass through the midst of you. . . . The end has come for My people Israel. I will spare them no longer. The songs of the palace will turn to wailing . . . [and] many will be the corpses. . . ."[12]

Micah

Micah also lived in a prosperous era, but it was a time marked by a precipitous disintegration of societal values and spiritual fidelity. God speaks not only to Judah but to each nation in revolt against Him—He says:

Behold I am planning against this family a calamity. . . . Then they will cry out to the LORD, but He will not answer them. Instead He will hide His face from them. . . . Because they have practiced evil deeds. . . . "I will execute vengeance in anger and wrath on the nations which have not obeyed. . . . Therefore, I will give you up for destruction."[13]

Zephaniah

Judgment was the central theme of the prophet's message—Immediate judgment at the hands of the foreign invader Nebuchadnezzar and God's ultimate reckoning at the end of the age. God says:

> "I will punish men who are stagnate in spirit." . . .Woe to her who is rebellious. . . . She did not trust in the LORD; she did not draw near to her God. . . . "Indeed, My decision is to gather nations. . . . To pour out on them My indignation, all My burning anger; for all the earth will be devoured by the fire of My zeal."[14]

Nahum

God pronounces His "melting hearts and knocking knees" condemnation upon Nineveh. Some sobering and powerful excerpts from Nahum 1 are included in the Prologue and are not repeated here. The prophet writes:

> Mountains quake because of [God] and the hills dissolve; indeed the earth is upheaved by His presence. . . . His wrath is poured out like fire. . . . "I will prepare your grave, for you are contemptible." . . .Hearts are melting and knees are knocking! Also anguish is in the whole body, and all their faces are grown pale! . . ."Behold, I am against you," declares the LORD of hosts. . . . Woe to the bloody city. . . . Many [are] slain, a mass of corpses and countless dead bodies. . . . Also her small children were dashed to pieces at the head of every street. . . . [15]

Habakkuk

Justice was nonexistent in Judah. Violence and wickedness permeated the culture. Through the prophet, God answers two weighty questions regarding His judgement of the guilty. One, He judges on His timetable alone. And two, He uses whatever instrument of judgement as seems good to Him. Yes, He's God. He does whatever He pleases, whenever He pleases, however He pleases. He gives no accounting of Himself in this regard. God judges Judah with a Babylonian sword, and then will exercise His prerogative to judge the instrument of His judgment, the Babylonians. God says:

> I am raising up the Chaldeans . . . that fierce . . . dreaded and feared [people] . . . [who] come for violence . . . [who] slay nations without sparing . . . he is like death, never satisfied. . . . Woe to him . . . [he] will become plunder. . . . Woe to him who builds a city with bloodshed. . . . Woe to you . . . you will be filled with disgrace. Before Him goes pestilence and plague comes after Him. . . . He looked and startled the nations, yes, the perpetual mountains were shattered the ancient hills collapsed. The mountains saw You and quaked. . . . In indignation You marched through the earth. In anger You trampled the nations.[16]

Zechariah

The prophet describes an obstinate people who, through their own willful stubbornness and sin, had lost the ear of God. The prophet writes:

> "And they made their hearts like flint so that they could not hear the law and the words which the LORD of hosts had sent by His Spirit through the former prophets; therefore great wrath came from the LORD of hosts. And it came about that just as He called and they would not listen, so they called and I would not listen," says the LORD of hosts. . . . [17]

Isaiah

God's man brings a word of "avenging" condemnation upon the vacuous religiosity of the day that included blatant idolatry. Isaiah foresaw both the consequent catastrophe of Judah being carried into captivity by the Babylonians as well as God's end-times judgment. Some powerful excerpts from Isaiah 13 are included in the Introduction and are not repeated here. Isaiah writes:

The Mighty One of Israel declares, "I will be relieved of My adversaries and avenge Myself on My foes. . . . For the LORD of hosts will have a day of reckoning . . . Woe to them! For they have brought evil on themselves. . . . For they have despised the word of the Holy One. . . . On this account the anger of the LORD has burned. . . . The earth will be completely laid waste. . . . All joy turns to gloom. The gaiety of the earth is banished. Terror and pit and snare confront you, O inhabitants of the earth."[18]

For behold, the LORD is about to come out from His place to punish the inhabitants of the earth for their iniquity. . . . Burning is His anger . . . His lips are filled with indignation, and His tongue is like a consuming fire. . . . Trembling has seized the godless. . . . For the LORD's indignation is against all nations . . . the LORD has a day of vengeance...According to their deeds so He will repay, wrath to His adversaries, recompense to His enemies.[19]

"I also trod them in My anger and trampled them in My wrath; and their lifeblood is sprinkled on My garments. . . . For the day of vengeance was in My heart." . . .He shall be indignant toward His enemies. For behold, the LORD will come in fire. . . . To render His anger with fury and His rebuke with flames of fire. For the LORD will execute judgment by fire and by His sword on all flesh, and those slain by the LORD will be many. . . . "Then they shall go forth and look on the corpses of the men who have transgressed against Me. For their worm shall not die, and their fire shall not be quenched. . . . "[20]

Ezekiel
Ezekiel did much of his prophetic work as an exile in Babylon. He spoke graphically of both Israel's and Judah's mutiny against God which led to their subjugation. Consider God's exhortation and warning to all mankind through His prophet—Yahweh says, "He who hears, let him hear; and he who refuses, let him refuse. . . . "[21]

I am against you. . . . My eye shall have no pity and I will
not spare. . . . Thus my anger will be spent, and I will satisfy My wrath on them. . . . I will make you a desolation
. . . an object of horror to the nations who surround you,
when I execute judgments against you in anger, wrath,
and raging rebukes . . . and I shall send My anger against
you; I shall judge you according to your ways. . . . A disaster, [a] unique disaster, behold it is coming! All hands
will hang limp and all knees will become like water . . .
and though they cry in My ear with a loud voice, yet I
shall not listen to them.[22]

"Utterly slay old men, young men, maidens, little children, and women. . . . My eye will have no pity. . . . I shall
bring their conduct upon their heads. . . . My four severe
judgments against Jerusalem: sword, famine, wild beasts
and plague. . . . I will make the land desolate. . . . I shall
bring on you the blood of wrath and jealousy. . . . I shall
enter into judgment with you face to face . . . and every
heart will melt . . . and you will know that I, the Lord,
have poured out My wrath on you. . . . I have consumed
them with the fire of My wrath; their way I have brought
upon their heads. . . . For thus says the Lord God, '. . .[I]
give them over to terror and plunder.'[23]

I, the Lord, have spoken; it is coming, and I shall act.
I shall not relent, and I shall not pity, and I shall not
be sorry; according to your ways and according to your
deeds I shall judge you. . . . And I will execute great
vengeance on them with wrathful rebukes. . . . I shall
bring terrors on you. . . . Wail, the day of the Lord
is near. . . . A time of doom for the nations. . . . I will
make Myself known among them when I judge . . . I
poured out My wrath on them. . . . My fury will mount
up in My anger. And in My zeal and in My blazing
wrath . . . all the men who are on the face of the earth
will shake at My presence . . . and they will know that
I am the Lord.[24]

Jeremiah

In the face of cruel opposition, the "weeping prophet"[25] faith-fully proclaimed God's doom on an apostate and idolatrous Judah. The Babylonian juggernaut would be God's immediate instrument of disaster. Additionally, there are multiple allusions to God's judgement at the end of the age. Jehovah says through his prophet:

> And I will pronounce My judgments on them concerning all their wickedness, whereby they have forsaken Me and have offered sacrifices to other gods, and worshiped the works of their own hands. . . . [You have] walked after emptiness and become empty. . . . Have you not done this to yourself by . . . forsaking the LORD your God?. . . Yet My people have forgotten Me. . . . Behold I will enter into judgment with you. . . . [Repent] lest My wrath go forth like fire and burn with none to quench it . . . . And all the cities were pulled down. . . before His fierce anger. . . . Shall I not avenge Myself?[26]

> Hear O earth; behold, I am bringing disaster on this people. . . . Behold, My anger and My wrath will be poured out on this place . . . it will burn and not be quenched . . . . Behold, terror!. . . They refuse to know Me. . . . I will send the sword after them until I have annihilated them. . . . At His wrath the earth quakes, and the nations cannot endure His indignation. . . . Though they will cry to Me, yet I will not listen. . . . There is no peace for anyone. . . . Because of the fierce anger of the LORD . . . I will not show pity nor be sorry nor have compassion that I should not destroy them.[27]

> . . .for I shall pour out their own wickedness on them. . . . I shall appoint over them four kinds of doom. . . . And I shall make them an object of horror. . . . I will suddenly bring down on her anguish. . . . For a fire has been kindled in My anger, it will burn upon you . . . which will burn forever. . . . Behold, I am fashioning calamity

against you. . . . I Myself shall war against you with an outstretched hand and a mighty arm, even in anger and wrath and great indignation. . . . The storm of the LORD has gone forth in wrath. . . . I will utterly destroy them and make them a horror. . . . [28]

And those slain by the LORD on that day shall be from one end of the earth to the other . . . because of the fierce anger of the LORD. . . . Behold the tempest of the LORD! Wrath has gone forth. . . . The fierce anger of the LORD will not turn back. . . . Behold, I am going to set My face against you for woe. . . . I am going to bring disaster on all flesh. . . . Terror on every side . . . a day of vengeance . . . a slaughter for the LORD God. . . . Behold, I am going to bring terror upon you. . . . For the LORD is a God of recompense, He will fully repay.[29]

Wrath and Weeping

Jeremiah mourns God's overthrow and destruction of Jerusalem by means of the Babylonians. Following are some select words, phrases, and verses that flowed from the prophet's pen in the book known as Lamentations.

. . .lonely, like a widow, weeps bitterly, none to comfort, harsh servitude, distress, mourning, desolate, groaning, afflicted, bitter. For the LORD has caused her grief because of the multitude of her transgressions . . . homelessness, despised. Look and see if there is any pain like my pain which was severely dealt out to me, which the LORD inflicted on the day of His fierce anger . . . desolate, crush, trodden, no one to comfort, pain, calamity. . . . In the day of His anger the Lord . . . has not spared. . . . In His wrath He brought them down. He has poured out His wrath like fire.[30]

The Lord has become like an enemy. . . . Mourning and moaning. He has despised king and priest in the indignation of His anger . . . He has not restrained His hand

from destroying . . . He has thrown down without sparing. Should women eat their offspring?...Terrors on every
side . . . there was no one who escaped or survived in the
day of the LORD's anger. He has caused my flesh . . . to
waste away. He has . . . encompassed me with bitterness
and hardship. Even when I cry out . . . for help, He shuts
out my prayer. . . . He is to me like a bear lying in wait.
He has . . . torn me to pieces. He has made me desolate.[31]

You have covered Yourself with anger. And pursued us;
You have slain and have not spared. . . . Panic and pitfall
have befallen us, devastation and destruction . . . My eyes
pour down unceasingly. . . . You will recompense them,
O LORD, according to the work of their hands. You will
give them hardness of heart, Your curse will be on them.
You will pursue them in anger and destroy them. . . . The
hands of compassionate women boiled their own children. They became food for them. The LORD has accom-
plished His wrath, He has poured out His fierce anger.[32]

A Full-Disclosure God

So, what's left to say?

One sure deduction would be that if you still don't believe
the biblical God is a God of great wrath, vengeance, recompense,
and terror—you either have an acute reading-comprehension-
learning impairment or, you simply prefer to delude yourself
with one of the illusion gods referenced earlier. But again, just to
remind you, your mythical god will be conspicuously absent on
that last day. You will not stand before him or her. You will stand
before the "terrifyingly magnificent"[33] God who is. The God who
has given you His Self-revelation in the Bible—the God who has
infallibly spoken through His prophets concerning His righteous
retribution for all who are in rebellion against Him. You will meet
Him face to face. You will look Him in the eye. You will then, inescapably and forever, believe with every fiber of your being in a
dangerous God.

Thankfully, Yahweh is a full-disclosure God. We're not left to
grope for truth in a vacuum. He has spoken. The Bible is clear. He

is a magnificent Savior and, yes, He is a fearsome Judge. Again, He will be glorified as both. And just one more reminder, God is not seeking your approval regarding who He is and how He metes out the "wages of sin"[34] in judgment. Your input is neither needed nor desired. God is simply revealing Himself to any and all who will "hear."[35]

Pure Delight and Comprehensive Horror

The God who is, blesses. And, He ruins. He gives, and, in judgment, takes away. He brings eternal joy, and, by judicial decree, infinite terror. Hear His prescient words to the Exodus Jews regarding their eventual rebellion against Him. This passage clearly reveals His proficiency as both a benevolent provider and an indignant judge. God says through His prophet:

> And it shall come about that as the LORD delighted over you to prosper you, and multiply you, so the LORD will delight over you to make you perish and destroy you. . . .[36]

Yes, God gives life, and He kills.[37] He is pure delight and comprehensive horror. He is faithful to His Word concerning both. This is always the Potter's right as He is pleased to display His glory in both His kindness and severity.[38] And to any remaining critics of Jehovah regarding His holy justice employed against mankind's rebellion, I will simply quote His prophet: "Why should any living mortal, or any man, offer complaint in view of his sin?"[39]

✍

*"You have slain them in the day of Your anger,
You have slaughtered, not sparing."*[40]
Jeremiah, God's Prophet

NOTES

1 Ezekiel 7:3, 7.
2 Matthew 23:13-33 (excerpts).
3 John 8:44.
4 Isaiah 30:9-10.
5 2 Timothy 4:3-4.
6 Jeremiah 5:31, 6:10, 5:3, 6, 9, 22, 6:12.
7 John Piper, Sermon, Bethlehem Baptist Church, Minneapolis, MN.
8 Ibid.
9 Obadiah 1:4, 9, 10, 15, 18.
10 Joel 1:8-11, 13, 15, 17, 2:1-3, 6, 11.
11 Hosea 5:4, 6-7, 7:13, 9:9, 10:14, 13:16.
12 Amos 3:6, 8, 5:17, 8:2-3.
13 Micah 2:3, 3:4, 5:15, 6:16.
14 Zephaniah 1:12, 3:1-2, 8.
15 Nahum 1:5-6, 14, 2:10, 13, 3:1, 3, 10.
16 Habakkuk 1:6, 7, 9, 17, 2:5-7, 12, 15-16, 3:5-6, 10, 12.
17 Zechariah 7:12-13.
18 Isaiah 1:24, 2:12, 3:9, 5:24-25, 24:3, 11, 17.
19 Isaiah 26:21, 30:27, 33:14, 34:2, 8, 59:18.
20 Isaiah 63:3-4, 66:14-16, 24.
21 Ezekiel 3:27.
22 Ezekiel 5:8, 11, 13-15, 7:3, 5, 17, 8:18.
23 Ezekiel 9:6, 10, 14:21, 15:8, 16:38, 20:35, 21:7, 22:22, 31, 23:46.
24 Ezekiel 24:14, 25:17, 26:21, 30:2-3, 35:11, 36:18, 38:18-20, 39:6.
25 Jeremiah 9:1, 13:17, 14:17.
26 Jeremiah 1:16, 2:5, 17, 32, 35, 4:4, 26, 5:29.
27 Jeremiah 6:19, 7:20, 8:15, 9:6, 16, 10:10, 11:11, 12:12-13, 13:14.
28 Jeremiah 14:16, 15:3, 4, 8, 14, 17:4, 18:11, 21:5, 23:19, 25:9.
29 Jeremiah 25:33, 37, 30:23-24, 44:11, 45:5, 46:5, 10, 49:5, 51:56.
30 Lamentations 1:1-5, 7, 11-13, 15, 17-18, 21, 2:1-2, 4.
31 Lamentations 2: 5-6, 8, 17, 20, 22, 3:4-5, 8, 10-11.
32 Lamentations 3:43, 47, 49, 64-66, 4:10-11.
33 John Piper, *Spectacular Sins* (Wheaton, IL: Crossway, 2008), 13.
34 Romans 6:23.
35 Ezekiel 3:27.
36 Deuteronomy 28:63.
37 1 Samuel 2:6.
38 Romans 11:22.
39 Lamentations 3:39.
40 Lamentations 2:21.

seven

9 TEACHINGS OF JESUS CHRIST

God's Eternal Sentence

*". . .fear the One who . . . has authority to cast into hell;
yes, I tell you, fear Him!"*[1]
Jesus Christ, God Incarnate

The very worst thing about the temporal judgments of God
chronicled in the book thus far is that they're not only temporal.

> **Temporal** *adj.* 1. Pertaining to, concerned with, or lim-
> ited by time. 2. Pertaining to or concerned with worldly
> affairs. 3. Enduring for a short time; short-lived. . . . [2]

God's historical decrees against the rebellion of mankind
do indeed appear to be in keeping with the above definition.
At first glance, they do, in fact, look to be "limited by time"
and "short-lived." However, His judicial verdicts in time are
merely inaugural. His fierce adjudications upon the earth are
only the beginning of an unending, omnipotent avalanche of
divine fury. More wrath is coming. Infinitely more. Everlastingly more.

The very worst thing about the final judgment Jesus Christ
repeatedly spoke of is that it is the antithesis of temporal. It is not
"limited by time" or "short-lived." It is eternal.

> Eternal *adj.* 1. Without . . . end; existing outside of time. 2. . . .without interruption or end. 3. Unaffected by time; timeless. 4. ...endless; interminable.[3]

It will be helpful to keep these two words and their definitions in the forefront of your mind as you read and consider this chapter regarding the teachings of Jesus Christ concerning final judgment—specifically, His teaching on eternal, conscious punishment in hell. You must seek to let your mind's eye adjust to a kind of timeless farsightedness, or you will never begin to feel the weight of the Son of Man's words. We're all living on the edge of eternity. Forever is but one heartbeat away. Suffice to say, understanding Messiah's teaching here matters far more than anything else you've got going on right now.

A Billion Eternities Overflowing with Wrath

In the first six chapters of the book, we've witnessed several of the historical judgments of God. He is unwavering regarding His holy and just response to the insurrection of man. We have seen Him unleash divine wrath, vengeance, recompense, and terror over and over again upon His enemies in the context of time. The Bible reveals, however, that the horror of temporal judgment is but a faint glimmer of that which is to come—namely, divine indignation beyond the grave. God's eternal fury is, as the definition makes clear, without end, timeless, endless, interminable. You must stop and ponder this. God's wrath, like Himself, is infinite. It is everlasting. Yes, perpetual and never-ending. After a billion eternities, God's anger will have only just begun to be poured out. God means for you to understand that this is a fixed reality in the cosmos. This is not religious myth or ecclesiastical bluff. Infinite outrage awaits every unrepentant soul. Provoked holiness knows no bounds. Renown, eighteenth-century American theologian, Jonathan Edwards, gives us some perspective here. Regarding the occupant of hell, he writes:

> It would be dreadful to suffer this "fierceness and wrath of Almighty God" (Revelation 19:15) for just one moment; but you must suffer for all eternity. . . . You will know

without question that you must wear out long ages, millions and millions of ages, in wrestling and conflicting with this almighty, merciless vengeance...You will absolutely lose all hope . . . of ever having any deliverance, any end, any mitigation, any rest at all. . . . [And] when so many ages have actually been spent by you in this manner, you will know everything you have suffered is but a pinpoint compared to what remains. Your punishment will indeed be infinite.[4]

An Indispensable Doctrine

Jesus Christ said that wrath, vengeance, recompense, and terror are forever. To reiterate, by definition, they are without end, timeless, endless, interminable. Why am I belaboring this point? Because you must work hard to begin to feel it. While none of us ever fully arrives in this regard, we must seek to comprehend this reality to the degree that our finite hearts and minds will allow. If you do not attempt to grasp the scope, meaning, purpose, and implications of Christ's words in this respect, you will

» Never begin to get even some limited sense of His unapproachable holiness and "terrifying magnificence."[5] Consequently, you will not fear God as He intends and as you must. The depth of your worship and your view of His longsuffering grace toward you will be unavoidably retarded.

» Never begin to regard your sin as you must—as a monstrous, horrific, personal insult directed at your awesome, fearsome, consuming-fire Creator-God, and deserving of infinite punishment. King David employed no hyperbole as he wrote, "Against You, You only, I have sinned."[6]

» Never begin to plumb the truly unfathomable height, breadth, and depth of Christ's finished work on the cross on your behalf. Consequently, your single-minded adoration, praise, devotion,

commitment, obedience, and love for the Savior
will be unavoidably diminished.

What's at stake in a deep understanding of the doctrine of
hell? Nothing less than a right comprehension of your God, your
worship, your sin, and His cross. Yes, a biblical understanding
of hell matters every day you roll out of bed. A true disciple of
Christ is utterly hamstrung without it. Sure, there's a lot of chat-
ter in the pseudo-church discounting hell, but there is no intellectually honest way to escape the obvious meaning of the Lord's
words on this topic. Words matter. Words mean what they mean.
The Son of God was never ambiguous. Never. Without question,
eternal conscious punishment is the most hated doctrine in the
Bible, but it is the indisputably clear teaching of God incarnate.
Hell is real. It is forever. Jesus Christ said so.

A Hell-Fire Preacher
If you know your Bible, it is no surprise to you that we learn
more about hell from the lips of Jesus than from any other biblical source. Regarding judgment and hell, noted contemporary
Christian scholar John Blanchard writes,

> Jesus spoke more about these two topics than about any
> other . . . [and] that of about forty parables Jesus told,
> more than half of them relate to God's eternal judgment
> of sinners . . . of the twelve times that the word *Gehenna*,
> the strongest biblical word for "hell", appears in the New
> Testament, there is only one occasion when Jesus was
> not the speaker.[7]

In a very broad stroke summary, Jesus Christ said hell is real.
He said it is eternal. It is terrible. It is deserved. And once there,
it is inescapable. According to Jesus, hell is:

- That place where "there shall be weeping and
  gnashing of teeth"—Matthew 13:42.
- "The furnace of fire"—Matthew 13:50.
- "The outer darkness"—Matthew 25:30.

- "Eternal fire"—Matthew 25:41.
- "Eternal punishment"—Matthew 25:46.
- An "unquenchable fire"—Mark 9:43.
- A place "where their worm does not die"—Mark 9:44, 46, 48.
- A place where "everyone will be salted with fire"—Mark 9:49.
- "Torment" and "agony" with a "fixed chasm" preventing escape—Luke 16:23-25, 26.

The Obvious Question

Embedded within the words of Jesus, in short, we hear that hell is a place of darkness, rage, despair, banishment, separation, loneliness, deprivation, loss, suffering, decay, distress, guilt, pressure, affliction, anguish, suffering, confinement, wretchedness, contempt, misery, shame, hopelessness, fire, pain, curse, ruin, torment, agony, and horror, etc., etc., etc.!

If Jesus Christ was so painstakingly clear about the reality and nature of hell, it raises the obvious question: Why does the religious professional at the church you attend never mention any of this? You know why. Everyone knows why. Because there's a better chance you'll be back in attendance next Sunday if your pseudo-minister creatively edits God. Sounds bad, I know. But maybe it's time to be honest with yourself, and about that "church" you've been attending. Either Jesus Christ is God, and everything He said matters as much as anything possibly ever could. Or, He is a fraud and His words are utterly inconsequential. I simply invite you to have some intellectual integrity here. Make a call on this. Is He God or not? Does He speak truth or not? Does what He says about hell matter or not? And, if it does matter, how can you stay in that so-called church that never, and I mean never, mentions Jesus' teachings on hell? This is an urgent question for you, your family, and everyone else sitting in the faux church you're attending.

Self-Pity and Rage

It's interesting that the phrase Jesus used most often (seven times) to describe the sinner in hell is that of "weeping and gnashing of teeth." What is the Lord telling us? In his weeping, doubtless the occupant of hell is utterly self-consumed with his own hopeless plight. This weeping is not about remorse and repentance. These are tears of self-pity. He is not sorry for his rebellion; he is only sorry for its consequence. No doubt the gnashing of teeth not only connotes the pain of the inhabitant of hell but also his extreme anger. Rage is the better word. So, who is the object of this ire? While there is certainly an acute self-loathing involved, as well as an ardent hatred for everyone else confined there, principally the rage of the resident of hell is directed at God.

The rebel hated God in this life[8] and hell has not changed that. In fact, hell has deeply intensified that emotion. Hell is not redemptive. It only amplifies natural man's loathing of the biblical God. As has been said many times, it is in hell that the baseline truth about mankind is plainly and finally revealed. It's the point I think C. S. Lewis is getting at as he describes the damned as successful rebels to the end, with the doors of hell being locked on the inside.[9] And this means, theoretically (for it is not possible for the condemned to come out of hell), that while utterly miserable, the tenants of hell would not come out *if* the precondition for doing so was to genuinely love God with all their heart, soul, mind, and strength.[10] They hate Him with every fiber of their being. And with every passing nanosecond in hell, they hate Him all the more!

God in Hell

There's another kind of rage in hell. That is, God's infinite wrath, anger, and vengeance. The biblical God is omnipresent. He is, by self-description, in hell. David tells us that if he makes his bed in "hell"[11] God is there. The Bible's most frequent description of hell is that of fire. Roughly twenty different passages in both the Old and New Testaments refer to fire in describing hell. In Scripture, fire is a recurring phenomenon in the manifest presence of God. In His fiery ferocity, God is in hell. Through Moses' pen, God says, "For a fire is kindled in My anger, and shall burn to the lowest hell. . . ."[12] The prophet tells us that, "The breath of the LORD, [is] like a torrent of brimstone. . . ."[13] The psalmist sings, "Fire goes before Him and burns up His adversaries round about."[14] The Holy Spirit reveals that, "God is a consuming fire."[15] And regarding God's presence in the punishment of the wicked, the apostle records that the rebel

> will be tormented with fire and brimstone in the presence of the holy angels and in the presence of the Lamb.[16]

Based upon 2 Thessalonians 1:9, many often describe hell as "eternal separation" from God. Blanchard helps us here. He writes:

> We tend to think of separation in terms of distance; the Bible speaks of it in terms of relationship. In hell, the sinner will not be separated from God in the sense that he will not see Him or know of His existence; instead he will live forever in His awesome presence . . . it might be more helpful if we thought in terms of alienation.[17]

Yes, the alienation *is* the separation. God in all His infinite fury is present in hell. As seventeenth-century English theologian John Favel writes, "The worst terrors of the prisoners in hell come from the presence of the Lamb"[18]—the angry Lamb,[19] as the apostle reminds us. Adds nineteenth-century English preacher Charles Spurgeon, "it seems more a wonder to meet . . . God in hell than in heaven. . . . Of course the presence of God produces very different effects...the bliss of one, the terror of the other."[20] God is there—terrifyingly so. There are no atheists or agnostics in hell.

Read It Like an Eight-Year Old

Again, as always, words, grammar, and context matter. As I think Francis Chan said somewhere, all you need to do to understand the Bible is to read it like an eight-year old. You know, just a simple reading of the text, without a personal agenda or ideological clutter. Just letting the words mean what they mean. Following are a few texts that convincingly point to the eternality of punishment in hell for all who are sent there:

Daniel 12:2—". . .many of those who sleep in the dust of the ground will awake . . . to everlasting life, but the others to disgrace and everlasting contempt."
Matthew 18:8—". . .it is better for you to enter life crippled or lame, than having two hands or two feet, to be cast into the eternal fire."
Mark 9:42-48—"[hell is] where their worm does not die, and the fire is not quenched."
2 Thessalonians 1:9—"These shall be punished with everlasting destruction . . . " (NKJV)
Jude 7—". . .since they . . . indulged in gross immorality and went after strange flesh, [they] are exhibited as an example, in undergoing the punishment of eternal fire."

If our eight-year-old possesses no more than average comprehension skills, the above texts are quite persuasive. The following texts profoundly advance the argument:

Revelation 14:9-11—"If anyone worships the beast . . . the smoke of their torment goes up forever and ever; and they have no rest day and night . . . "
Revelation 20:10, 14-15—"And the devil . . . was thrown into the lake of fire and brimstone, where the beast and the false prophet are . . . and they will be tormented day and night forever and ever. . . . This is the second death, the lake of fire. And if anyone's name was not found written in the book of life, he was thrown into the lake of fire."

In the unlikely event our eight-year-old is not yet fully convinced, the next text, from the lips of Jesus, puts an end to any legitimate debate regarding eternal, conscious punishment for lost mankind. Notice how the Lord's comment here ties damned humanity's fate to that of the devil and his minions in the lake of fire as mentioned above in Revelation 20:10,14-15. In the final judgment, God incarnate will speak these words to all who have persisted in their rebellion against Him:

Matthew 25:41, 46—". . .depart from Me, accursed ones, into the eternal fire which has been prepared for the devil and his angels. . . . And these will go away into eternal punishment, but the righteous into eternal life."

Yes, damned humanity will be cast into the lake of fire with the devil and his angels whom the Revelation text reminds us are "tormented day and night forever and ever."

Moreover, in the Matthew 25 text, it is important to note that the same Greek word translated *eternal* is used to describe both punishment and life beyond the grave. If we understand that in the phrase "eternal life," Jesus is talking about life eternal—namely, everlasting existence, being, and animation . . . which is of course how we understand what He is saying—how is it then possible to not understand "eternal punishment" in exactly the same light—specifically, that the tenants of hell have existence, being, and animation in the midst of eternal punishment? Certainly, it is not possible for those with a modicum of intellectual integrity. Our eight-year-old readily understands, as does everyone else who deals honestly with this text, that the debate ends right here. The Bible categorically teaches eternal conscious punishment for every impenitent human soul.

Interestingly, the writer of Hebrews powerfully underscores the rule of the eight-year-old for us by reminding us that "eternal judgment" is in fact an "elementary teaching."[21] Obviously, this teaching of Jesus is not complicated, nor in any way difficult to interpret or understand; it's just that it is hated by those who abhor the invincible holiness and just retribution of an infinitely incensed God.

"You Thought I Was Just Like You"
Granted, eternal conscious punishment is a weighty biblical truth—one that plainly crushes our finite capacities to even begin to comprehend all that it portends. Clearly, that fact alone is not a valid argument against the Son's unambiguous teaching. Certainly, thoughtful Christians can and do struggle with this truth, but the true believer never dares question the righteousness of God in the face of this doctrine's overwhelming scope.

Ultimately, He's God and we're not. He does not need or seek our counsel in any aspect of His cosmic administrations, much less His holy verdict against rebellious men. With all empathy and humility, I simply ask—what exactly did you expect from the thrice, and yes, fiercely holy I AM WHO I AM[22] Sovereign Creator-God of heaven and earth? Did you expect a wrath the finite mind could easily accommodate? Did you expect a damnation more in keeping with fallen human sensibilities? Unquestionably, it is one of mankind's gravest miscalculations as God has affirmed through His psalmist, "You thought that I was just like you. . . ."[23]

Temporal Sin = Eternal Punishment?

One of the most common objections to eternal conscious punishment is the fact that our sin, committed in time, is forever punished. 78.69 years of sin is punished everlastingly. The math is a problem for some. There are two fairly obvious reasons that punishment for sin committed in the context of finite time necessarily leads to a never-ending sentence in hell.

First and principally, our sin is against eternal and infinite God. Consequently, the punishment for such offense is inescapably eternal and infinite. Edwards helps us here. He writes:

> The crime of one being, despising and casting contempt on another, is proportionately more or less heinous as he was under greater or less obligations to obey him. . . .
> Therefore, if there be any being that we are under infinite obligations to love, honor, and obey, the contrary towards him, must be infinitely faulty. . . . God is a being infinitely lovely because he hath infinite excellency and infinite beauty. So, sin against God, being a violation of infinite obligations, must be a crime infinitely heinous, and so, deserving of infinite punishment. The eternity of the punishment of ungodly men, renders it infinite and, therefore, renders it . . . no more than proportionable to the heinousness of what they are guilty of.[24]

Secondly, and often overlooked, is the fact that the occupant of hell never stops sinning. He sins everlastingly. As a moral creature in premeditated rebellion, proactively hating God with all his being, he never ceases to be guilty before the Creator—forever. His temporal antipathy toward God follows him into eternity. His perpetual sin perpetually fuels the eternality of his hell. The doctrine of eternal, conscious punishment is not only crystal clear biblically, but it is logically unavoidable. Considering who God is and the rebellion of mankind against Him, nineteenth-century American theologian W. G. T. Shedd is right in saying, "If there were no hell in Scripture, we should be compelled to invent one."[25]

Impugning the Son
In reaction to Jesus' blunt, graphic, and horrifying description of eternal damnation, many false teachers have sought to simply dispense with the obvious meaning of His words. The three most prominent attempts to save the impenitent from eternal conscious punishment are:

> **Universalism**—All mankind is saved unconditionally.
> **Universal Restoration**—At death, or after some appropriate time in hell, the resurrected body and soul are redeemed.
> **Annihilationism**—At death, or after some appropriate time in hell, the resurrected body and soul go out of existence.

So, there is only one small problem with these arguments. They are wholly bereft of any biblical support. In fact, each, in one way or another, flatly contradicts the words of the Son of God. They are demonstrably heretical. As someone somewhere said, if any of these propositions is true, Jesus Christ was either an incompetent theologian, or He was a liar. Yeah, there is just a whole lot at stake with the biblical doctrine of hell in more ways than one. To in any way diminish Christ's teaching in this regard, or to subscribe to any of the false assertions above, is to emphatically impugn the character and trustworthiness of God incarnate . . . no small matter!

The Symbolism Conjecture

And just a quick word on the symbolism conjecture. There are many who seek to moderate the impact of the graphic images the Bible uses to describe hell. They tell us that "fire" is only a metaphor, an analogy, a symbol. This kind of talk will not suffice. It will not get you where you want to go. When, in human language, is the symbol ever more than the reality? The symbol is used for the very reason that the reality cannot be sufficiently verbalized.

Regarding the ghastly images the Bible uses to describe hell, contemporary American theologian Jim Elliff says that these are "signposts to something worse." He continues, "What if the true hell can only be experienced, and not described?"[26] Without question, Elliff is on to something here for this is the obvious sense one gets when reading the descriptions of hell in the Bible. In short, the horrors and terrors of hell cannot in any conceivable way be overstated. Hell is ultimately beyond human description. What is breathtakingly true for those who love God, specifically, that human eye has not seen, nor human ear heard, nor human heart conceived, all that God has prepared for those who love Him,[27] is equally and terrifyingly true for those who hate Him.

The Mirror, or God

In one sense, apprehending the biblical teaching on hell comes down to our principal focus. If we are only looking at ourselves and mankind in general, we tend to inevitably "feel" that eternal conscious punishment does not seem just. It is simply far too severe. Consequently, we conclude, the Bible could not possibly be teaching it. In looking in the mirror alone, it is easy to convince ourselves that hell does not seem appropriate in the circumstance. However, if we are genuinely looking at the pristine holiness, the uncompromising righteousness, and the absolute justice of the awesome, reigning Creator-God in Scripture, we are otherwise compelled to say—since God incarnate, Jesus Christ says eternal conscious punishment is a fact—it must not only be just, it must be necessary.

Therefore, if Jesus Christ says that it is just, right, and necessary—how infinitely incomprehensible is the holiness of God. How infinitely blameworthy it must be to treat the glory of God with indifference or contempt. What infinite glory and purity God must possess that everlasting suffering is the fitting punishment for dishonoring and disobeying Him. Moreover, what a stunning, shocking, amazing, astonishing, unbelievable thing Jesus Christ has done in taking my sin and God's wrath upon Himself! As we will see in Chapter Nine, damnation is not the most outrageous doctrine in Scripture; salvation by grace alone, through faith alone, in Christ alone, is.[28]

Why Then Should You Not Suffer?

God means for you to believe what He has clearly revealed in His Word regarding hell. I believe it is the paramount lesson of the parable of Lazarus and the rich man in Luke 16 as told by Jesus Christ—namely, to heed the Word of God! The Lord taught that Lazarus died and went to paradise. The rich man also died and went to Hades. In torment and agony, the rich man cried out to Abraham, who was in the presence of God, for relief. Abraham responded that such assistance was not possible due the great chasm fixed between paradise and hell. Then the rich man asked Abraham if he might send Lazarus to warn his brothers so that they would not also come to this place of anguish. Abraham responded, saying:

"They have Moses and the Prophets; let them hear them."
But he said, "No, Father Abraham, but if someone goes to them from the dead, they will repent!" But he said to him, "If they do not listen to Moses and the Prophets, neither will they be persuaded if someone rises from the dead."[29]

Jesus is saying, "Let them hear the Word of God!" This is the bottom-line message here and in this book. Yes, let each man be careful to hear, believe, and intelligently respond to God's revelation concerning hell. If a person is unwilling to heed God's clear warning of eternal conscious punishment in the Scriptures, there is no hope for such obstinacy. Yes, let all men everywhere hear the Word of God!

And to every person who will not—every person who willfully despises Jesus Christ and His clear teaching . . . or has insulted Him with heart-dead, rote religion . . . or has simply been indifferent toward Him—twentieth-century English theologian A. W. Pink replies, "Why then should you not suffer wrath as great as that grace and love which you have rejected?"[30]

$\mathscr{G}$

"Who understands the power of Your anger and Your fury, according to the fear that is due You?"[31]
Moses, God's Prophet

NOTES

1   Luke 12:5.
2   "Temporal," *The American Heritage Dictionary* (Boston: Houghton Mifflin Co., 1985).
3   "Eternal," *The American Heritage Dictionary* (Boston: Houghton Mifflin Co., 1985).
4   Jonathan Edwards, *Sinners in the Hands of an Angry God,* (New Kensington, PA: Whitaker House, 1997), 56-57.
5   John Piper, *Spectacular Sins* (Wheaton, IL: Crossway, 2008), 13.
6   Psalm 51:4.
7   John Blanchard, *Whatever Happened to Hell?* (Durham, England: Evangelical Press, 1993), 128-129.
8   Romans 1:30.
9   C. S. Lewis, *A Year with C.S. Lewis* (San Francisco, CA: HarperCollins, 2003), 367.
10 Mark 12:30.
11 Psalm 139:8 (NKJV).
12 Deuteronomy 32:22 (NKJV).
13 Isaiah 30:33.
14 Psalm 97:3.
15 Hebrews 12:29.
16 Revelation 14:10-11.
17 Blanchard, 161.
18 Cited in Blanchard, 160.
19 Revelation 6:16.
20 Charles H. Spurgeon, *The Treasury of David, Vol 3* (Peabody MA: Hendrickson Publishers, 1988), 261.
21 Hebrews 6:1-2.
22 Exodus 3:14.
23 Psalm 50:21.
24 Cited by John Piper, Sermon, *The Echo and Insufficiency of Hell*, Resolved Conference, Palm Springs, CA.
25 Cited in Blanchard, 148.
26 Jim Elliff, "My Darkest Night; Hopefully Not Yours," Christian Communicators Worldwide, April 9, 2013, accessed June 6, 2019, http://www.ccwtoday.org/article/my-darkest-night-hopefully-not-yours/#sthash.G2DttBv8.dpuf.
27 1 Corinthians 2:9.
28 Portions of this paragraph adapted from John Piper, Sermon, Bethlehem Baptist Church, Minneapolis, MN.
29 Luke 16:29-31.
30 A. W. Pink, *Studies in the Scriptures—1922-23, Vol. 1,* (Lafayette, IN: Sovereign Grace Publishers, 2001), 113.
31 Psalm 90:11.

eight

66ᴛʜ Book

God's End-Times Judgment

"Terror is on every side. . . . "[1]
Jeremiah, God's Prophet

You can't read God's sixty-sixth book and not feel it. The terror that is. Dread and horror fill the pages of God's final book. It's Yahweh's promise to all who have willfully made themselves His enemy.

God says, "Vengeance is Mine, I will repay. . . . "[2] His prophet adds, "The recompense of God will come. . . . "[3] Yes, it is coming. For at the end of the age, John tells us that *all* men *everywhere* will cry out to the mountains and the rocks, "Fall on us and hide us from the presence of Him who sits on the throne, and from the wrath of the Lamb, for the great day of their wrath has come; who is able to stand?"[4] If you've read the 66th book, you know that no impenitent person will stand in the face of God's omnipotent fury. Indeed, as the apostle writes, they will prefer suicide to standing before the angry Lamb. But death is no escape. It is only the beginning of infinite terror. Lamb-phobia is no exaggerated dread. The angry Lamb is the consummate human horror! And there will never be any escape from His terrifying presence—forever!

This Chapter's Goal

It is not the intent of this brief chapter to parse the cryptic particulars of Revelation. That is way above my pay grade. My goal is simple: for us to feel, at least in some very limited sense, the weight, sweep, and scope of God's premeditated and unwavering wrath reserved for this damned planet and unrepentant humanity. Jeremiah is right, as noted above: when God unleashes His final wrath, there will be terror on every side.

To begin our look at this prophetic book, it seems good to revisit our subtitle. Remember, these are God's words—not mine. It's how Jehovah describes His holy response to those who are in revolt against Him. The sixty-sixth book is replete with:

> **Wrath** *n.* 1. Violent . . . anger; rage; fury. 2. b. Divine retribution for sin.

> **Vengeance** *n.* 1. The act or motive of punishing another in payment for a wrong or injury he has committed; retribution. 2. With great violence or fury.

> **Recompense** *n.* 2. To . . . make return for. Amends made for something, as damage or loss. Payment in return for something given or done. . . .

> **Terror** *n.* 1. Intense, overpowering fear. 2. Something, as a terrifying object or occurrence, that instills intense fear. 3. The ability to instill intense fear.[5]

Each of these—wrath, vengeance, recompense, and terror—is the rebel's guaranteed inheritance from God as He brings human history upon this disposable world to a close. These are the unrepentant sinner's wages. Again, God is invincibly faithful. He always delivers on a promise. He can be trusted to render all that is due to every last insurgent. The LORD says through His prophet, "For the day of vengeance was in My heart. . . ."[6] So it is, as is historically evident from the pages of Scripture. And yes, some may be very surprised to learn that this divine vengeance is, in fact, the fervent prayer of heaven.

An Answered Prayer

So, what are the holiest of saints in heaven praying about—those who were martyred for their faithfulness to the Word of God? What are they praying for? Your average church member would never guess. I mean, they would never, ever guess. John tells us these holy ones are praying for one thing—vengeance! "How long O Lord, holy and true, will You refrain from judging and avenging our blood on those who dwell on the earth?"[7] Jesus Christ said it, ". . .shall not God bring about justice for His elect, who cry to Him day and night, and will He delay long over them? I tell you that He will bring about justice for them speedily."[8] God has promised His just vengeance. It is inevitable and inescapable. He assures His people that He will not tarry long.

Of course, in our day, a proper church member from your average congregation would never pray such a prayer. It would be beneath them. Certainly, it would be improper in polite company and without question, insufficiently religious, virtuous, and pious. For the nominal Christian, vengeance talk is not only unpleasant, it is overtly offensive. It's the sub-biblical, post-Christian, contemporary view of God which portrays Him as merely love; only love . . . nothing but love. Honestly, isn't it only those annoying fundamentalists who talk about God's vengeance? What do those unrefined, literalist rubes know anyway? I guess, the Bible.

God's Glory in His Spent Wrath

Adding to the contempt your average church member has for this heavenly petition is the sub-biblical, post-Christian, contemporary view of what a real Christian is supposed to look like. I mean, if the drive to church is the riskiest part of your Christianity, you cannot begin to fathom this prayer, nor of course, would you have any need of it. Only true believers love this prayer. Only one who is being conformed to the image of the Son[9] gets what this is all about. Only one with an unadulterated thirst for God's righteousness to shine forth comprehends this. Only one who has tasted the hostility and distain of the God-hating world grasps it. Only one who desires to see God glorified in rendering His pristine justice truly values this—for His vengeance will put His holiness on display for all to see!

Every true disciple of Christ knows that with God's final judgment, the wicked will be eternally cast off, ushering in everlasting righteousness for the redeemed in the new heavens and new earth. Yes! As David sings! In all these things, "The righteous man will be glad. . . . "[10] Amen! We will be very, very glad when God unleashes His conclusive fury! No true believer pretends to be more longsuffering and compassionate than God. We, like our Father, have a taste for this—for the glory of God in His spent wrath. Yes, we will eagerly join the multitudes of heaven in singing "Hallelujah! Hallelujah!" as God "avenges the blood of His bond-servants"[11] and deals "out retribution to those who do not know God . . . and do not obey the gospel. . . . "[12]

So yes, God loves this avenging prayer from His people. The genuine disciple knows this is ultimately all about Yahweh and the integrity of His Word. Holy God will see to it. All moral accounts will be exquisitely settled. You're right, your average denominational god would never entertain such a prayer or ever talk about something as distasteful to the typical church member as vengeance. But again, as noted more than once in this book thus far, the god of your average church today is the figment of some religious professional's imagination. All pseudo-christs will be conspicuously absent on the last day. Only the angry Lamb will be in view. Every eye will be on Him as He meticulously and fiercely answers the heavenly prayer for vengeance.

Not Our Job

Parenthetically, vengeance is not our job. This is God's right alone. The Bible makes this clear for every follower of Jesus Christ. Back to the Romans 12 text quoted a few paragraphs ago. God says to every professed Christian:

> Never take your own vengeance, but leave room for the wrath of God, "Vengeance is Mine, I will repay," says the Lord. "But if your enemy is hungry, feed him, and if he is thirsty, give him a drink; for in so doing, you will heap burning coals upon his head." Do not be overcome by evil but overcome evil with good.[13]

Vengeance is not ours. It's God's. He says, "It is Mine." So, we're to leave it alone. Born-again believers seek to honor God and His Word relative to this challenging command. While this is never easy, we submit to His mandate. It's what real disciples do. As Peter writes, we must refuse to "return evil for evil or insult for insult but [give] a blessing instead."[14] It's how God has called His "aliens and strangers"[15] to live in this world. But, when God begins to draw the final curtain on this condemned globe and the billions of God-rejecting rebels living on it, we will rejoice in His holy wrath. We will heartily agree with God's actions and His angels' proclamation, "Fear God, and give Him glory, because the hour of His judgment has come. . . . "[16] Close parenthesis.

So What?

It's the response of some in the so-called contemporary church to John's Revelation. Yeah, so what? At best, the book is labeled as allegory, metaphor, or parable. At worst, its dismissed altogether as myth, legend, or fable with absolutely no real-life application for postmodern man. Obviously, there is much that could be said here. I will simply point out two textual realities for the skeptic's consideration.

First, it would serve us well to remember John's description of the One[17] who gave him this revelation. He was no ordinary person—no commonplace prognosticator. To the contrary, He was so "terrifyingly magnificent"[18] that, when John saw Him, he fell at His feet as a dead man.[19] John described Him as

> . . .one like a son of man . . . girded across His breast with a golden girdle. . . . And His head and His hair were white like white wool, like snow; and His eyes were like a flame of fire; and His feet were like burnished bronze . . . and His voice was like the sound of many waters. And in His right hand He held seven stars; and out of His mouth came a sharp two-edged sword; and His face was like the sun shining in its strength.[20]

Yes, He is the One that "myriads of myriads, and thousands of thousands"[21] worship in heaven, saying with a loud voice:

"Worthy is the Lamb that was slain to receive power and riches and wisdom and might and honor and glory and blessing." And every created thing which is in heaven and on the earth and under the earth and on the sea, and all things in them, I heard saying, "To Him who sits on the throne, and to the Lamb, be blessing and honor and glory and dominion forever and ever."[22]

So what? So, this—Jesus Christ is God and He is "coming quickly"[23] in fierce wrath! He is the One who has given this prophecy! Believe it, or don't. But reader, you have been properly cautioned. Omnipotent, vengeance-is-on-my-heart God is speaking to you!

Secondly, is the unique and stunning warning to all who hear or read the sixty-sixth book. Regarding God's end-times revelation, John writes that

. . .if anyone adds to them, God shall add to him the plagues which are written in this book, and if anyone takes away from the words of the book of this prophecy, God shall take away his part from the tree of life. . . . [24]

So what? So, this—Jesus Christ is God and He is coming to crush His enemies! He has promised His omnipotent curse upon any man who would manipulate, spin, negate, ignore, or disparage His warning of final judgment upon mankind. Believe it, or don't. But you have been duly warned. The biblical God is an I-will-repay Promise-Keeper!

Where Judgment Begins
In the early chapters of Revelation, God begins with His professing church. It's what the Lord told us through Peter's pen which is really the perfect entrée into the sixty-sixth book for both the believer and the unbeliever.

For it is time for judgment to begin with the household of God; and if it begins with us first, what will be the outcome for those who do not obey the gospel of God? And if it is with difficulty that the righteous is saved, what will become of the godless man and the sinner?[25]

So yes, God begins His final book with those called by His name. He directly addresses seven churches. Five are, to say the least, falling short. Ephesus had left its "first love."[26] Pergamum and Thyatira were tolerating sin.[27] Sardis was, in the Lord's words, "dead," in need of repentance—for there were but a "few" true believers.[28] And last, was the infamous church of Laodicea—the only church to which God has nothing good to say.

Laodicea is an atrophied church. A Laodicean-type church today still bears the name Christian, but it doesn't really believe much of anything anymore. It still uses biblical words and concepts, but it is mostly religious routine. It still meets on Sunday, but most members don't honestly remember why. The church in Laodicea professed to be rich, and in fact they were in a material sense, but spiritually, God said they were wretched, miserable, poor, blind, and naked.[29] Christ says:

I know your works, that you are neither cold nor hot. I could wish you were cold or hot. So then, because you are lukewarm, and neither cold nor hot, I will vomit you out of My mouth.[30]

God Gags

Could the Lord be any clearer? The lukewarm church member makes Him sick! He or she makes God gag! Sadly, Laodicea is a picture of the pervasive reality in the modern era. Many professing Christians are so utterly immersed in simply doing church for the sake of doing it, that they are oblivious to the fact that Christ will not receive their muddled and contrived worship. It is hollow. It's all show and no go. Such churchgoers profess some sort of belief in Christ, but do not know Him or love Him. They belong to a purported church and attend semiregularly, but they do not obey the Lord in the world. Jesus' half-brother said it perfectly. Real Christians prove themselves to be "doers of the word, not merely hearers who delude themselves."[31] Even the casual observer of the modern church can plainly see that millions who profess Christ are deceived in their lukewarm religiosity.

Francis Chan quantifies it perfectly. He writes, "Something is wrong when our lives make sense to unbelievers."[32] It's what lukewarm Christianity always looks like. The average professed Christian's life in the twenty-first century looks exactly like that of his unbelieving neighbor apart from the inconvenience of his somewhat sporadic church attendance. Laodicea is the rule in this era. Nominal is the new normal. And even though the biblical God has been expelled from the pseudo-church bearing His name, He calls her to repentance. Shockingly, Jesus Christ depicts Himself as standing at the door of the Laodicean church, knocking, waiting for someone, anyone, to let Him in.[33]

Christ told us it would be like this—that there would indeed be tares among the wheat.[34] He said there would be pseudo-Christians amid the true believers in the visible church. He told us there would be a harvest of wrath from the professing church. Concerning both false and true disciples, Messiah said:

> Allow both to grow together until the harvest . . . [and] the Son of Man will send forth His angels, and they will gather out of His kingdom all stumbling blocks, and those who commit lawlessness, and will cast them into the furnace of fire; in that place there shall be weeping and gnashing of teeth.[35]

The Day of the Lord

The Day of the Lord is a technical term in Scripture connoting an indeterminate season of God's overt judicial intervention in history. "Day of the Lord" proclamations in the Bible can have both imminent and future fulfillments. Regarding Revelation, the day of the Lord is not to be understood as a literal day, but a specific time at the end of the age that Yahweh has set aside to execute His righteous vengeance upon all usurpers, both angels and men.

In order to get a sense of the cataclysmic upheaval of this final judgment, it seems wise and good, and ultimately most effective, to pick out words, phrases, verses, and passages the Holy Spirit has given us in Revelation to describe the fierce wrath God has promised His enemies. These are His words—God's words. The apostle writes:

> . . .behold an ashen horse and he who sat on it had the name Death; and Hades was following after him. And authority was given to them over a fourth of the earth, to kill with sword and with famine and with pestilence. . . . And there was a great earthquake; and the sun became black . . . and the moon became like blood; and the stars of the sky fell to earth . . . and every mountain and island was moved out of their places. . . . And there followed peals of thunder and sounds and flashes of lightning and an earthquake. . . . And there came hail and fire . . . and a third of the earth was burned up. . . . A third of the sea become blood. . . . A third of the rivers and . . . springs of water . . . became bitter and many men died from the waters...[36]

> And a third of the sun and . . . moon . . . and stars were . . . darkened. [Demonic beings were loosed from the pit but] were not permitted to kill anyone but to torment [the ungodly]. . . . In those days, men will seek death and will not find it; and they will long to die and death flees from them. And . . . four angels . . . were released, so that they might kill a third of mankind . . . by three plagues, And . . . [men] will drink of the wine of the wrath of God, which is mixed in full strength in the cup of His anger; and [they] will be tormented with fire and brimstone . . . forever and ever.[37]

> [And in the judgments of God, men] "gnawed their tongues because of the pain and they blasphemed the God of heaven because of their pains and their sores. . . . And there were flashes of lightning and . . . peals of thunder; and there was a great earthquake, such as there had not been since man came to be upon the earth . . . pestilence, mourning and famine . . . woe, woe . . . for in one hour your judgment has come . . . torment, weeping,

and mourning . . . woe, woe . . . in one hour such great wealth has been laid waste!³⁸

And I saw heaven opened, and behold, a white horse, and He who sat on it is called Faithful and True, and in righteousness He judges and wages war. His eyes are a flame of fire, and on His head are many diadems; and He has a name written on Him which no one knows except Himself. He is clothed with a robe dipped in blood, and His name is called The Word of God. And the armies which are in heaven, clothed in fine linen, white and clean, were following Him on white horses. From His mouth comes a sharp sword, so that with it He may strike down the nations, and He will rule them with a rod of iron; and He treads the wine press of the fierce wrath of God, the Almighty. And on His robe and on His thigh, He has a name written, "KING OF KINGS, AND LORD OF LORDS."³⁹

And I saw a great white throne and Him who sat upon it, from whose presence earth and heaven fled away, and no place was found for them. And I saw the dead, the great and the small, standing before the throne, and books were opened; and another book was opened, which is the book of life; and the dead were judged from the things which were written in the books, according to their deeds. And the sea gave up the dead which were in it, and death and Hades gave up the dead which were in them; and they were judged, every one of them according to their deeds. Then death and Hades were thrown into the lake of fire. This is the second death, the lake of fire. And if anyone's name was not found written in the book of life, he was thrown into the lake of fire.⁴⁰

Ultimate Cosmic Realities
So, what is the compelling message of God in His sixty-sixth book? Judgment is coming. It cannot be avoided. It is inevitable. It's the promise and purpose of God. Yes, Jonathan Edwards was

right—God has had it on His heart to show to angels and to men how terrible His wrath is! How many will perish in the end-times judgment of God? Billions. How many will be damned? Billions. This offends you? Oh, I see. Are you still thinking that you're more compassionate than God? I counsel caution here. Jesus Christ is God and you're not. Better learn to accept and ultimately rejoice in God's pristine justice or you will certainly have no part in His grace and mercy. He doesn't run His universe to please His creatures. He "works all things after the counsel of His will . . . to the praise of His glory."[41] He will be glorified in the redemption of His people and He will be glorified in the damnation of His enemies. These are ultimate cosmic realities for humanity.

The sixty-sixth book is unambiguous. Jesus Christ is coming. Judgement is coming. Wrath is coming. Vengeance is coming. The second death is coming. This will happen. "Every eye"[42] will see it. You will see it. And you will delight in His vengeance as do the saints in heaven or you will be swept into hell by it. It's your call, for God has provided a remedy for any and all who would repent and believe . . . just turn the page.

ℒ

"Woe, woe, woe, to those who dwell on the earth. . . ."[43]
John, God's Apostle

NOTES

1 Jeremiah 6:25.
2 Romans 12:19.
3 Isaiah 35:4.
4 Revelation 6:16-17.
5 All definitions are from *The American Heritage Dictionary* (Boston: Houghton Mifflin Co., 1985).
6 Isaiah 63:4.
7 Revelation 6:10.
8 Luke 18:7-8.
9 Romans 8:29.
10 Psalm 64:10.
11 Revelation 19:1-3.
12 2 Thessalonians 1:8.
13 Romans 12:19-21.
14 1 Peter 3:9.
15 1 Peter 2:11.
16 Revelation 14:7.
17 Revelation 1:18.
18 John Piper, *Spectacular Sins* (Wheaton, IL: Crossway, 2008), 13.
19 Revelation 1:17.
20 Revelation 1:13-16.
21 Revelation 5:11.
22 Revelation 5:12-13.
23 Revelation 22:12.
24 Revelation 22:18-19.
25 1 Peter 4:17-18.
26 Revelation 2:4.
27 Revelation 2:14-15, 20-21.
28 Revelation 3:1, 3-4.
29 Revelation 3:17.
30 Revelation 3:15-16. (NKJV).
31 James 1:22.
32 Francis Chan, *Crazy Love* (Colorado Springs, CO: David C. Cook Publishing, 2008), 115.
33 Revelation 3:20.
34 Matthew 13:24-30, 34-42.
35 Matthew 13:30, 41-42.
36 Revelation 6:8, 12-14, 8:5, 7-11.
37 Revelation 8:12, 9:3-6, 15, 18, 14:10-11.
38 Revelation 16:10-11,18, 18:8, 10, 15-17.
39 Revelation 19:11-16.
40 Revelation 20:11-15.
41 Ephesians 1:11-12.
42 Revelation 1:7.
43 Revelation 8:13.

nine

6 Hours

God's Remedy

"For Christ also died for sins . . .
in order that He might bring us to God. . . . "[1]
Peter, God's Apostle

We won't come to God—without God. We have no desire for God—apart from God. We don't want God. Not really. If we are to ever come to God, we must be brought to God by God. Apart from our Creator invading our lives, rescuing us from ourselves, and bringing us to Himself, we will forever remain His enemy. It's what God says. It's who we are. It's the core truth of Peter's words noted above.

Some readers may protest. Some may believe that you sought God on your own. Some feel like you took the initiative to become the spiritual person you are. You may have made a decision for Christ. You may have asked Jesus into your heart—yeah, that non-biblical, incantation-like prayer. You may have been baptized. You might regularly attend the worship services of a respectable denomination. But I'm talking about the root issue for every human being. I'm asking you to be brutally honest with yourself—to take a long hard look in the mirror. Seeing as the subtitle of this book are the very words of God; this really does matter. It matters a lot. It matters forever. This is likely the most important question you've ever been asked to consider. I caution you—don't just parrot what you know you're supposed to say. Maybe for the first time in your life, think deeply about this and be truthful.

Here's the bottom-line question—Aren't you truly more interested in someone, or something, or some accomplishment, or some recognition, or some acquisition, or some security, or some comfort, or some experience, or some worldly pleasure than you are in God? Isn't this who multitudes of professed Christians really are, despite all the church-going and Jesus-talk? I pray this is not true of you, but in light of the stakes, as narrated in this book, isn't it worth some serious reflection?

A Shocking Reality

It's a shocking reality! It truly is hard to believe that humanity is genuinely more fascinated with some created thing or some temporal experience than with its Creator. As noted in some detail in Chapter Two, this is stunningly and universally true. God's apostle affirms it. He bluntly writes, ". . .There is none who seek for God."[2] Yes, that's all of us. Considering our chosen and premeditated alienation from God, we desperately need Someone to bring us to Him. To reconcile us to God. To resolve the wrath, vengeance, recompense, and terror problem that we all have. There is only one Someone who can—Jesus Christ. Again, we're talking about the biblical Jesus, not the pseudo-christs preached in many so-called churches every Sunday morning. The Bible is soberingly clear—God the Son and God the Spirit must bring us to God the Father, because we will not otherwise seek, nor come to Him. Scripture is alarmingly blunt: left to our own devices, we would all land in hell. This is who we are. This is biblical truth. We are utterly damned without His overture, without His coming, without Him atoning for our sins, without Him regenerating us, without God bringing us to God!

Stunned, Staggered, Breathless Awe

And there He is. He's in that manger. God is in a manger. Unsought. Unsolicited. Uninvited. Unwanted. Mankind's Savior conceived by the Spirit and born to two nobodies in a nowhere place. God in a body. Emmanuel, God with us. Yes, it is breathtaking. Stunningly so for anyone who thinks about it for more than thirty seconds. You're right—this does change everything forever. He obviously matters more than anyone or anything else possibly ever could. To paraphrase nineteenth-century English preacher Charles Spurgeon, this Son of Mary and Joseph is—Infinite, yet infant . . . eternal, yet born . . . almighty, yet suckled . . . upholding a universe, yet lying in a manger. Contemporary theologian J. I. Packer sums it up perfectly, as he writes, ". . .the more you think about it, the more staggering it is." If you're not genuinely staggered, you've not really understood it. If you're not stunned, you've not truly believed it. The Alpha and Omega Creator-God is in a manger! The galaxy-breathing-galaxy-sustaining God is in a manger! I-AM-El-Shaddai God is in a manger! Let the whole created order and every thinking, sentient being in it, stand in stunned, staggered, breathless awe! God has come to save His people from their self-absorbed selves!

First Things, First

So, how would you respond to this question? Why is He there? Ultimately, why is God in a manger? The Bible is crystal clear on the why. But sadly, your average preacher almost never fails to infer that God is there because it's all about you and me. Because you and I are just that important to God. Because we're uppermost in the heart and mind of God. If that is how your preacher preaches it, he is biblically illiterate and shouldn't be allowed anywhere near a pulpit. God has done all things, particularly the salvation of His people, as the prophet wrote, ". . .for the glory of God."[3] God said He claimed Israel as His own to "show My glory."[4] God chose the Jewish nation that they might be for Him "a people for renown, for praise, and for glory."[5] This divine initiative to save is, as the apostle repeatedly tells us, "to the praise of His glory."[6] Yes, Jesus Christ has come to redeem a people out of death and hell. Yes, He loves us like that.[7] But this saving of sinners is, first and foremost, about the glory of God and is "to the praise of the glory of His grace."[8] Chiefly, He saves, "for the sake of His name. . . . "[9] Jesus prayed it as He faced the cross, "Father, glorify your name."[10]

If you think God took on flesh and was crucified principally because of you, you've been utterly misinformed. As contemporary theologian Joe Rigney writes, "God is the most God-centered person in the universe. . . . God is no idolater; He will have no other gods before Him."[11] The Triune God treasures the Triune God above any and all—and yes, that of course means above you and me. God is eternally uppermost in the heart and mind of God. That's really, really, good news forever for every born-again soul, given that God is our reward.[12] Think about it.

A Preacher's Confession

I know you wouldn't expect such a confession from a preacher, but here it is. I've never much liked preaching on Christmas and Easter. I know that's sounds a bit strange, but I have my reasons. These biblical realities are just too big. The manger and the Cross are just so overwhelmingly huge. Every self-aware preacher knows he can't get there, no matter how erudite or eloquent he may be. There is no way to legitimately get there. There is absolutely no way to preach God's coming in the flesh and His saving work adequately. There is no way to sufficiently expound on the regenerating work of the Holy Spirit. It is simply not possible to fathom and communicate the staggering profundity of it all. Truly, it's like we should just lie on our faces for an hour on Christmas and Easter; as well as every other Sunday of the year! It's what I never fail to feel as I think deeply about God in a manger and God on a cross.

If you've read this far, you know we all have an insurmountable problem with an exceedingly dangerous God—an urgent problem none of us can solve. The first three verses of Ephesians 2 tell us that we are damned. God tells us we are spiritually dead, captive to Satan, and, by nature, children of wrath.[13] In response to our dilemma, the very next verse begins with two of the most beautiful words ever recorded. "But God. . . . " But God what? "But God, being rich in mercy, because of the great love with which He loved us . . . made us alive together with Christ. . . . "[14] God is our remedy. God came that He might bring us to God. God made a way. He didn't staff this out. In love, He came to make the dead, alive—to set the captive free—to expunge the wrath we deserve. He's in that manger because He is going to the Cross to save a people for the glory of His name! No man has ever preached these truths in any way vaguely approaching a worthy manner!

A Predestined Remedy

Obviously, Genesis 3 didn't catch God unawares. He knew man would rebel. If the god you worship doesn't know what the free-will choices of his creatures will be, well then, you have a cartoon-god. The God who is, made provision for His glory to be clearly manifested in the salvation of His people. When did God essentially save them? Before creation! The apostle is un-equivocal. He writes that God, "chose us in Him [Jesus Christ] before the foundation of the world. . . . He predestined us to adoption as sons through Jesus Christ. . . . For whom He fore-knew, He also predestined . . . and whom He predestined, these He also called; and whom He called, these He also justified; and whom He justified, these He also glorified."[15] Was the coming and crucifixion of the Son an *ad hoc*, stop-gap, eleventh-hour remedy for an unforeseen decision of man? No! It was a done deal on the far side of eternity past! For indeed, the Son of Man was "delivered up by the predetermined plan and foreknowl-edge of God."[16]

Who was in on the murder of Jesus Christ? Yes, the Jews. Yes, the Gentiles. But principally, this was the plan of Triune God. What men of their own free will meant for evil, God meant for good. Men of their own free, depraved, rebellious wills mur-dered the Son of God. God, of His own free, gracious, loving will, redeemed His people. Ultimately, God the Father did not spare His own Son but delivered Him up[17] Ultimately, God the Son laid His life down of His own initiative.[18] This was God's idea. The crucifixion of God was a God-ordained, God-decreed, God-planned, God-initiated event. The Son didn't lose control of events. He didn't get backed into a corner and end up on the cross. With resolute and unwavering premeditation, Jesus Christ went to the cross. He told Pilate, "For this I have been born."[19]

The Right Question

One reason, among many, I hate counterfeit gospels is that they very often evoke the question of *"Why me?"* Those who attend man-centered churches invariably hear about an emasculated god from a truncated biblical message. Such teaching often abets the hearer in seeing himself as a victim. Such an environment tends to produce self-absorbed, narcissistic, never-ending questions of—*"Why me?"* Man-centric, therapeutic gospels inevitably lead to an unhealthy preoccupation with self. Obviously, this is not God's intent. He is not in the business of making it all about man. Nor is He in the least bit interested in answering all of our "why" questions.

If we've read, understood, and believed our Bibles, we know *"Why?"* is always the wrong question. *"What?"* is the most pressing and urgently necessary question for every human being subject to the rage and fury of a dangerous God. It was the question the Philippian jailer put to the apostle Paul, "What must I do to be saved?"[20] While Yahweh doesn't answer a lot of *"Why?"* questions, He has made sure we know the answer to the *"What?"* question. In His gracious mercy, He has historically, powerfully, comprehensively, and emphatically answered the *"What?"* question. *"Who?"* is the answer to the *"What?"* question? "What must I do to be saved?" It's all about the *"who."* It's all about Jesus Christ. With respect to the *"Who?"* question, the apostle leaves no doubt. Regarding Jesus Christ, Peter preached, ". . .there is salvation in no one else; for there is no other name under heaven that has been given among men by which we must be saved."[21]

I Dare You Not to Worship

So . . . I'm going to tell you the story. Yeah, I know you know it. I know it's like *Muzak* to many readers . . . you know, like background music. That's why I'm going to tell you the story—again. The "Muzak" phenomenon is inexcusable on every possible level considering who Jesus Christ is, what He's done, and what He's promised. If you're a "Muzak" Christian, you need to repent! Right now! I pray you will read the "old, old story"[22] with fresh eyes. That you would hear it again, as if it were the first time.

That you would endeavor to deeply feel the breathtaking awe of the single most horrific and single most magnificent moment in the history of the cosmos! This is God's remedy to the looming wrath, vengeance, recompense, and terror problem all the sons and daughters of Adam have before their Creator. God has come to be butchered for His bride. I invite you to read it—again. And, if you will take the time to deliberately and genuinely take it in afresh and anew . . . I dare you not to worship!

God on a Donkey

Here He comes. God-incarnate on a donkey. He's coming to bring us to God. He will sacrifice Himself. He will give Himself over to a brutal scourging and crucifixion. Let's take a moment to remember just exactly who is riding into Jerusalem on this lowly beast. He is Yahweh. He said it multiple times in numerous ways and they hated it every time—but He just kept saying it. Jesus Christ said, "Truly, truly, I say to you, before Abraham was born, I am."[23] He said, "I and the Father are one."[24] He said, "He who has seen Me has seen the Father. . . . I am in the Father, and the Father is in Me."[25]

The God who spoke a two-trillion galaxy cosmos into existence is on that donkey. The God who formed man from the dust of the ground. The God who commissioned Noah and swept away the rest of humanity. The God who unleashed fire and brimstone on Sodom and Gomorrah. The God who utterly crushed Egypt, killing every firstborn. The God who terrified Moses and the exodus Jews at Mount Sinai. The God who annihilated the Canaanite peoples. The God Isaiah saw. The God who devastated an apostate Israel and Judah in judgment. The awesome, fearsome, consuming-fire God of Psalms 97 and 99 . . .

> The LORD reigns let the earth rejoice. . . . Clouds and thick darkness surround Him; Righteousness and justice are the foundation of His throne. Fire goes before Him and burns up His adversaries round about. His lightnings lit up the world; the earth saw and trembled. The mountains melted like wax at the presence of the LORD, at the presence of the LORD of the whole earth. . . . The

LORD reigns, let the peoples tremble; He is enthroned above the cherubim, let the earth shake![26]

So why is Almighty, Sovereign, Creator God of heaven and earth riding a donkey through the gates of Jerusalem? You know. He's come to stage a cosmic intervention in the lives of usurpers, insurgents, and rebels. That's right—you and me. John writes, "For God so loved the world, that He gave His only begotten Son, that whoever believes in Him shall not perish, but have eternal life."[27] The Son has come for the Triune God's glory and for the joy of His ransomed people. Breathtaking!

God Arrested

Judas is on his way to betray Messiah while Jesus heads to the garden of Gethsemane. The Lord knows that Judas knows that's where He'll be. So, why does He go there? He's making it easy for Judas to earn his bounty. Ten times the religious leaders had sought and failed to arrest Jesus. Why will the eleventh attempt be successful? Because our Savior was born for this night, this place, this hour.

Matthew tells us that a "great multitude with swords and clubs"[28] came to arrest this Galilean carpenter. Jesus stepped between the wolves and His disciples and said, "Whom do you seek?"[29] His omniscience magnifies His courage. He knows what's going down. He's not in disguise. He's not hiding. He's not running. Yes, "The Lord is a warrior!"[30] They said they were seeking Jesus the Nazarene, and Christ responded, "I am." The entire arresting party fell to the ground from the sheer power of His Name.[31] Anyone with only average comprehension skills understands that this is no real arrest. They tie God up, but everyone knows who is in charge.

God Scourged and Rejected

Just as the arrest was a joke, so were the trials; all six of them. Ultimately, Jesus stood before the Roman governor, Pilate, who tried repeatedly to release Jesus for he could "find no guilt in Him."[32] Pilate sought to satisfy the Jewish religious leaders bloodlust by having God scourged.[33] It was a brutal and hid-

135

eous torture. The whip was made of braided leather strips with metal balls and pieces of sharp bone and/or metal shards woven into them. God was tied to a post and lashed thirty-nine times. His back, buttocks, and the back of His legs would have been shredded. Often the victim's back was so badly gashed that parts of the ribs, spine, veins, muscles, and even organs were sometimes exposed. The prophet wrote:

> "The chastening for our well-being fell upon Him and by His scourging we are healed" (Isaiah 53:5).

The Gospels tell us that after they scourged God, they put a crown of thorns on His head and clothed Him with a purple robe. Then they mocked God and hit God in the face. They spat on God and beat God on the head with a reed. And Pilate said, "Behold the Man!" And the chief priests and crowd cried out "Crucify, Crucify!" Pilate said, "Shall I crucify your King?" And the chief priests replied, "We have no king but Caesar."[34] Israel had utterly rejected her God and Messiah. The prophet had written:

> "Surely our griefs He Himself bore, and our sorrows He carried; yet we ourselves esteemed Him stricken, smitten of God, and afflicted" (Isaiah 53:4).

God Murdered

Crucifixion was so horrifying that many had to be dragged to their execution, but not Emmanuel. This was His design, His purpose, His "joy"[35]. The prophecy reads:

> "He was oppressed and He was afflicted yet He did not open His mouth; like a lamb that is led to slaughter. . . ." (Isaiah 53:7).

And the Bible records that they took Jesus to "Golgotha [and] there they crucified Him. . . ."[36] First, they stripped God naked. Then the Romans laid God down on the crossbeam. They took seven-inch spikes and drove them through God's wrists. Then they hoisted God vertically and drove spikes through His feet. As the vertical beam was dropped into a hole with a thud, both of God's shoulders dislocated. Once a man was hanging in the vertical position, he would normally die an agonizingly slow death by asphyxiation. Crucifixion was the slow annihilation of a man. Christ, however, would relinquish His spirit within hours. Yes, He is in control of it all. The prophet revealed that

"...the LORD was pleased to crush Him, putting Him to grief; If He would render Himself as a guilt offering..." (Isaiah 53:10).

Jesus is the guilt offering for His people. He took the full wrath, vengeance, recompense, and terror of God on that cross. He took what His people deserved. Our guilt fell to Him. His righteousness covers us. Paul writes, "He (the Father) made Him (the Son) who knew no sin to be sin on our behalf that we might become the righteousness of God in Him."[37] You must consider the bloody, brutal, savage cross long and hard. That's how ugly your sin is to God. That's what it cost Him to redeem you out of your depravity. It's a pristine picture of the wrath of God against your sin and mine being poured out upon the only One who could save us. Yes, those are our sin-wages. Isaiah wrote:

"But the LORD has caused the iniquity of us all to fall on Him" (Isaiah 53:6).

Mark tells us that Messiah was alive on the cross from the third hour to the ninth hour—a total of six hours.[38] Matthew tells us that darkness fell on the land from the sixth hour to the ninth hour evidencing God's curse upon the Son as His people's sins were laid upon Him. At about the ninth hour, Jesus said, "It is finished," and yielded up His spirit.[39] The prophecy reads that

"He poured out Himself to death, and was numbered with the transgressors. . . . He Himself bore the sin of many..." (Isaiah 53:12).

Parenthetically, back to all the *"Why?"* questions for a moment. Seriously, you're concerned with the petty *whys* in your life when God has provided the answers to the *"What?"* and the *"Who?"* questions? Here's a good *why* question to ponder. Ask yourself this—Why would a holy, righteous, and profoundly incensed Creator-God die for me, a self-made enemy of His? Now that's an exceedingly good *why* question, worthy of some serious contemplation. Close parenthesis.

God Resurrected
There are a lot of pseudo-intellectuals who deny the physical resurrection of Jesus Christ. I will not waste any time refuting them. This is simply a matter of believing what the Bible clearly asserts. The Scriptures affirm that Jesus appeared no fewer than ten times over a period of forty days to more than five hundred people. Ultimately, real Christians don't believe Christ is risen merely because of the objective physical evidences. Certainly, we rejoice in the biblical testimony as well as in the historical proofs and logical inferences that verify His resurrection; but that is not finally why we believe. We believe because of one undeniable and irrefutable fact. It's the very same reason Mary Magdalene believed.

It was early Sunday morning and Mary Magdalene was at Jesus' tomb. She was weeping for no good reason. She had much love, but no faith. This is one of the striking things about the resurrection of Christ—none of His followers expected it. They were the first skeptics. He'd told them numerous times that He would rise, but, ultimately, not one of them believed Him. Mary was crying, but Jesus had given her His promise that He would rise and yes . . . there He is. He asked her why she was weeping but she did not recognize Him. So how does Mary ultimately come to believe that Jesus had risen? Jesus said to her, "Mary!" Immediately, she knew it was her Savior! No one could speak her name like He could—full of God-sized love and intimacy![40]

You Do Not Believe Because You Are Not My Sheep
The Good Shepherd calls one of His sheep by name, and she knows! That's how every true believer knows. Genuine Chris-

tianity is never only about right doctrine. Satan believes the facts. It's always about a breathtaking God-encounter resulting in a life-changing, eternity-altering metamorphosis. It's always the "born-again"[41] work of the Holy Spirit—the blooming of the sacred romance. Biblical Christianity is not religion. It's relationship. Remember what Jesus told the religious leaders? He said, "You do not believe because you are not of My sheep."[42] A lot of people who call themselves Christians don't like it when God talks that way; but that's how He talks. The Lord said, "I am the good shepherd and I know My own and My own know Me . . . [and] My sheep hear My voice, and I know them, and they follow Me."[43] Mary immediately recognizes the voice of her Shepherd, the One who had laid "down His life for the sheep."[44] Jesus said:

> For this reason the Father loves Me, because I lay down My life that I may take it up again. No one has taken it away from Me, but I lay it down on My own initiative. I have authority to lay it down, and I have authority to take it up again . . . and I give eternal life to [the sheep], and they shall never perish; and no one shall snatch them out of My hand. My Father, who has given them to Me, is greater than all; and no one is able to snatch them out of the Father's hand.[45]

Jesus Christ came to save any and all who would repent of their sins and place their faith in Him as their Lord and Savior. Yes, in salvation God is sovereign and yes, in salvation you are responsible. You must exercise your will to escape the wrath, vengeance, recompense, and terror of God in judgement. The apostle wrote

> that if you confess with your mouth Jesus as Lord, and believe in your heart that God raised Him from the dead, you shall be saved; for with the heart man believes, resulting in righteousness, and with the mouth he confesses, resulting in salvation. For the Scripture says, "Whoever believes in Him will not be disappointed."[46]

Do You Really Believe?

Google tells me there are 2.2 billion people who profess to believe that God is in that manger in Bethlehem and on that cross in Jerusalem. At Christmas and Easter, multitudes of people pour into churches, many of whom attend only on those occasions. They profess to believe, but you can tell many really don't. You can tell because their former way of life is still their current way of life. Their so-called "before Jesus life" is mostly identical to their so-called "after Jesus life" except, as Francis Chan said somewhere, with a determined effort to "cuss less." You can tell that many don't truly believe because there is no life-altering awe, wonder, joy, worship, and obedience pouring out of their lives. If one truly believes that God is in that manger and on that cross, there is not one part of your life that will not be changed. You simply cannot genuinely believe the Christmas-Easter story in a lifestyle vacuum. There is no part of your life that will not be radically affected by those two historical realities.

If you really believe it . . . it will be way more than a semi-irregular-church-attendance kind of thing. In fact, it won't be religious at all. It will be an intensely personal thing. You will have met your Creator. You will have begun to know, love, trust, and obey Him. The relationship is real. It is intimate. It is dynamic. To really believe is to be utterly changed from the inside out. As every born-again Christian can testify, it is the only life worth living. It always manifests as a radical outward response to God's radical invasion of our lives. Eugene Peterson perfectly captures what this looks like in the true believer's life as he writes, "Take your everyday, ordinary life—your sleeping, eating, going to work and walking around life—and place it before God as an offering."[47] This is the life-style-offering of every true Christian.

A radically transformed life is the obvious and compelling truth of every born-again believer caught up in the Christmas and Easter stories. Nothing was ever the same for Mary, Joseph, the shepherds, and the magi at Christ's birth. And of course, nothing was ever the same for Mary Magdalene, Peter, James, John, and the rest at His resurrection. Sure, Satan and his minions believe. They believe so much that they tremble.[48] The test is never in merely believing the facts. The test is always in loving the Christ—delighting in Him and building your "walking around life" upon Him. He is your rock, your foundation.

So, do you really believe? Have you genuinely come to Jesus Christ and thus escaped the righteous wrath, vengeance, recompense, and terror of a justly incensed and dangerous God? God's apostle tells us how you can know:

> And by this we know that we have come to know Him, if we keep His commandments. The one who says, "I have come to know Him," and does not keep His commandments, is a liar, and the truth is not in him; but whoever keeps His word, in him the love of God has truly been perfected. By this we know that we are in Him: the one who says he abides in Him ought himself to walk in the same manner as He walked.[49]

ↄ

". . .how shall we escape if we neglect so great a salvation?"[50]
The Writer of Hebrews

NOTES

1   1 Peter 3:18.
2   Romans 3:11.
3   Isaiah 43:7.
4   Isaiah 49:3.
5   Jeremiah 13:11.
6   Ephesians 1:12, 14.
7   Romans 5:8.
8   Ephesians 1:6.
9   Psalm 106:8.
10   John 12:28.
11   Joe Rigney, "Why God Does Everything He Does," Desiring God, October 4, 2019, accessed October 5, 2019, https://www.desiringgod.org/articles/why-god-does-everything-he-does.
12   Genesis 15:1 (NKJV).
13   Ephesians 2:1-3.
14   Ephesians 2:4-5.
15   Ephesians 1:4-5, Romans 8:29-30.
16   Acts 2:23.
17   Romans 8:32.
18   John 10:18.
19   John 18:37.
20   Acts 16:30.
21   Acts 4:12.
22   "I Love to Tell the Story" (text by A. Catherine Hankey, music by William G. Fisher), The Baptist Hymnal (Nashville, TN: Convention Press, 1991), 572.
23   John 8:58.
24   John 10:30.
25   John 14:9, 11.
26   Psalm 97:1-5, 99:1.
27   John 3:16.
28   Matthew 26:47.
29   John 18:4.
30   Exodus 15:3.
31   John 18:5-6.
32   John 18:38.
33   John 19:1.
34   John 19:2-3, 5-6, 15, Matthew 27:30.
35   Hebrews 12:2.
36   John 19;17-18.
37   2 Corinthians 5:21.
38   Mark 15:25, 34-37.
39   John 19:30, Matthew 27:50.
40   John 20:11-16.
41   John 3:3.
42   John 10:26.
43   John 10:14, 27.
44   John 10:11.
45   John 10:17-18, 28-29.
46   Romans 10:9-11.
47   Romans 12:1 (The Message Bible).
48   James 2:19 (NKJV).
49   1 John 2:3-6.
50   Hebrews 2:3.

EPILOGUE:
YOU, AND THE WORD GOD HAS GIVEN

"But to this one I will look, to him who is humble, and contrite of spirit, and who trembles at My word."[1]

God

The Fool

The Bible says, "The fool has said in his heart, 'There is no God.'"[2] While not all cynics come right out and say the words, every skeptic with that unspoken sentiment wholly incarnates it in his or her life. It's an inviolable truth for each human being—the convictions of the heart always spill out into the life. Clearly, this is true for both the atheist and the one who is simply indifferent toward God. Biblically, there is no ultimate distinction between the militant unbeliever and the nominal believer. Both have shown themselves to be fools in that, as creatures, they have blasphemed their Creator with either their disdain or disinterest. Scripture goes on to say that such "a fool does not delight in understanding . . ."[3] and that the "natural man does not accept the things of the Spirit of God; for they are foolishness to him, and he cannot understand them, because they are spiritually appraised . . . . For the word of the cross is to those who are perishing foolishness. . . ."[4] The bottom-line truth here is that both God's detractors and His lukewarm followers find Him and His wisdom tedious, irrelevant, and, yes . . . foolish. Fool is the epithet of all in hell.

The Wise
The Bible says that "a wise man is he who listens to counsel."[5] If this book is nothing else, it is one strenuous and sustained effort at relaying sound biblical counsel. To borrow an oft-repeated phrase from God's Word, the scriptural guidance found herein is for those who have the "ears to hear."[6] Indeed, it is for those who are prudent to heed their Creator and flee from the wrath to come, through the atoning work of the Son. As the prophet noted, God will look to the one who is humble, contrite, and trembles at His Word. So, it raises the urgent and unavoidably obvious questions: Are you in fact humble and contrite before Him? Are you willing, yes, eager, to tremble at His Word?

> **Humble** *adj* 1. Marked by meekness or modesty in behavior, attitude, or spirit. 2. Showing deferential or submissive respect. 3. . . .unpretentious.

> **Contrite** *adj* 1. Repentant for one's sins . . . penitent.

> **Tremble** *verb* 1. To shake involuntarily, as from fear. . . . 2. To feel or express fear. . . .[7]

Wisdom's Beginning
Some readers may have been in church all their lives and never pursued, much less sought to incarnate, God's unqualified call in Isaiah 66:2 above. But, indeed, humility, contrition, and an awed eagerness to tremble before God and His Word should predominate in the genuine believer's life.

Regarding wisdom's genesis, *first*, the thinking person viscerally grasps that there must be an adequate First Cause, and Christians understand that the biblical God is the only viable candidate on the world's stage. There are no others. I dare you—go find me one. I AM is the One who effortlessly spoke a beautifully complex and seemingly infinite cosmos into existence. He is the One who creates dirt and then breathes life into it, creating a man. *Secondly*, and as we have seen, the Bible plainly teaches that our Creator is unapproachably holy—yes . . . consuming-fire, melting-hearts, knocking-knees holy![8]

Consequently, for the authentic Christian, humility before our transcendent, omnipotent Creator is not a problem. We are reflexively humble before the almighty Architect of all things! Likewise, before our invincibly holy Sovereign, we are contrite and repentant regarding our self-absorbed rebellion against Him. The Isaiah 66:2 injunctions are not a rational or logical challenge for us—in fact, they are intuitively necessary for anyone paying much attention at all. And yes, because of these realities, the thoughtful person *will* come to genuinely fear the Lord! Such overwhelming reverence is beyond merely instinctive; it is, as the wise king wrote, "the beginning of knowledge and wisdom."[9] Could there be a more self-evident, elementary, foundational, intellectual apprehension for the creature than the proper acknowledgement of and regard for the Creator? To tremble before God and His Word is no real stretch for the average IQ!

All Will Fear Him . . . One Way or the Other
And here is the unavoidable synthesis of biblical truth regarding the fear of the Lord—if you will not now gladly know that the Lord is God and fear Him as you must, you will ultimately know and experience that reality in great terror. It was one of the lessons Pharaoh's obstinacy taught us in Chapter Four. For indeed, you can fear your Creator the easy way—in humility, contrition, and reverence, or you can fear Him the hard way—as the end result of a self-glorifying, God-ignoring life. One path will bring you to eternal life, joy, and pleasure; the other, to eternal death, torment, and horror. It is one of God's immutable cosmic truths. Every person will know the fear of the Lord one way or the other—in heaven, or in hell. I don't believe it's presumptuous to say that wisdom is not difficult to discover here.

Ignorant Skeptics
Oh, I see, one of your many objections to this book is that it contains too much Bible. You don't really accept the Bible as the inerrant, infallible, authoritative Word of God. You're not comfortable with a God of wrath, vengeance, recompense, and terror. I get this a lot. But as you must know, once you discount the Bible, all you have left at best is human speculation, or worse, demonic

deception. You're right: the foregoing sentence is a distinction without a difference.

Concerning your average biblical skeptic, let me share that I've never personally encountered one who had actually put any effort into his conviction. In my thirty-five years of ministry, not one single scoffer had ever bothered to do his homework. Scoffers just never know what they're talking about. Yes, we're back to how your average fool insists on prosecuting his one, very short life upon this planet—despising divine wisdom, and preferring, instead, to rely purely upon his fallen intellectual assumptions and subjective feelings. So, what about the Bible?

The Bible—Its Claim!
The Bible literally claims to be the Word of God thousands of times in phrases like "The LORD God said. . . ."[10] and "Thus, says the LORD. . . ."[11] The Scriptures powerfully speak to some of its inherent characteristics. For example:

> "The grass withers, the flower fades, but the word of God stands forever."[12]

> God says, "So shall My word be which goes forth from My mouth; it shall not return to Me empty, without accomplishing what I desire, and without succeeding in the matter for which I sent it."[13]

> " . . .man does not live by bread alone, but man lives by everything that proceeds out of the mouth of the LORD."[14]

> " . . .until heaven and earth pass away, not the smallest letter or stroke shall pass away from the Law until all is accomplished."[15]

> God says, " . . .the Scripture cannot be broken."[16]

> "All Scripture is inspired by God."[17]

> " . . .no prophecy of Scripture . . . was ever made by an act

of human will, but men moved by the Holy Spirit spoke from God."[8]

The Bible—Like Any Other Book?

Most people say the Bible is a book like any other, possessing no inherent value or relevancy. This grossly uninformed assertion ignores that the Bible has supernatural written all over it—from beginning to end! The Bible is comprised of sixty-six books, written by forty different human authors over a period of 1,500 years, in three different languages, on three different continents, with a common story line, theme, and message, with no historical or factual errors, and no doctrinal contradictions. As one seminary professor aptly said, "Go find another book in the world like that." As his student rightly countered "That's impossible!" Yeah.

The Bible—Contains Error?

Many say the Bible contains truth, but also contains error and the mere opinions of primitive men. As is obvious, this position is, in the end, a commentary on the character and nature of the biblical God Himself. For in keeping with this assertion, the god behind a specious bible would have to be a pathetic kind of god who lost control of his revelation—a god who simply could not keep his creatures from hijacking his message. Clearly, this variety of god is no God at all, and we certainly need not be overly concerned with what he might have to say to us. If you are a reader who holds such a position, I would simply caution that I'm not sure there is a greater insult to your Creator than to portray Him in this light. Yes, in due course, He will teach every unbeliever that His Word is invincibly true!

Ultimately, you must either say that the god of a commandeered, flawed revelation is pitiable, warranting none of our attention . . . or, you must say that the God of the Bible is God and, consequently, His revelation to us is "more desirable . . . than much fine gold"[19] and, indeed, consists in the very "words of eternal life."[20] There is no plausible middle position here. If the God of the Bible is God, preserving His Word intact for us is a very small thing for Him to do. No, you don't get to play the middle with the Bible. You're either all in, or you're not in at all.

This is risky business, for no person of sound reasoning ventures to become El Shaddai's editor. Surely, the circumspect would never dare purport to be the final arbiter of God's truth. The true believer joyfully receives the biblical assertion that the Bible is "God-breathed"![21] In His Word, God has said what He means, and He means what He has said. Woe to the man who would presume to stand in judgment over the Living God's self-revelation, for surely that man is the quintessential definition of a fool.

The Bible—An Ocean of Evidence!

By some unknowably vast factor, the Bible is the most scrutinized book in the history of the world and yet has never been finally and credibly challenged in any valid field of study by any legitimate scholar. The scholarship has been done. It is irrefutable. We have an accurate copy of God's revelation in both the Old and New Testaments. Don't take my word for it; do your own research.

Apart from the Bible's textual evidences, including its internal consistencies, manuscript reliability and redundancy, there is an abundance of prophetic, historical, and archeological corroborations. Moreover, the Bible is where mankind encounters the Living God and where His people meet and come to love Him. Regarding this reality, John Piper preaches that "God's peculiar glory shines through His Word [and that] . . . in one self-authenticating sight, our mind is sure, and our heart is satisfied."[22] Translation: If you still have doubts about the integrity and veracity of the Bible, you've not yet met the One who gave it. It's true, your view of Scripture is a pristine reflection of your view of the God of Scripture. To disparage the Bible is to disparage your Maker. Do I need to say it? Your view of the Bible is a pretty big deal. The implications are . . . everlasting!

No Excuses!

If you have doubts about the authenticity and reliability of the Bible, again, I encourage you to roll up your sleeves and go to work. Do your homework. Don't be an ignorant skeptic. Don't run with the lemmings. Don't follow the herd down the broad road.[23] It is urgent that you resolve this question. Wrath, vengeance, recompense, and terror forever weigh in the balance. It's what God has clearly revealed in His Word. It's why I end this book with this ever-so-brief tutorial on the Scriptures. God has plainly spoken. Will you hear Him? Will you escape damnation? Will you receive the Son as your Savior? Or, will you come face to face with the "terrifyingly magnificent,"[24] dangerous, and incensed God who is, as His adversary? Will you face the angry-Lamb? Will you be subject to infinite wrath for a billion eternities? Again, through His revelation, the Creator has made full disclosure regarding mankind's dilemma and His breathtaking remedy for such. Consequently, the ball is squarely in your court. One thing is sure: there'll be no excuses on that last day.

Are You Standing on Rock or Sand?
God incarnate says:

> Therefore everyone who hears these words of Mine and acts on them, may be compared to a wise man who built his house on the rock. And the rain fell, and the floods came, and the winds blew and slammed against that house; and yet it did not fall, for it had been founded on the rock. Everyone who hears these words of Mine and does not act on them, will be like a foolish man who built his house on the sand. The rain fell, and the floods came, and the winds blew and slammed against that house; and it fell—and great was its fall.[25]

Where are you standing? On rock, or sand? Are you a wise man or a fool? It is not only evident today—it will be evident every single moment of forever.

"Why Should You Die?"
I close the book with a tender invitation from the God who is— the dangerous God; the God of infinite wrath, vengeance, recompense, and terror; the God who will eternally condemn all who reject His Son or blaspheme Christ by merely playing religion with Him. The Sovereign LORD God of heaven and earth says:

I was sought by those who did not ask for Me; I was found by those who did not seek Me. I said, "Here I am, here I am,' . . .I have set before you life and death, blessing and cursing; therefore choose life. . . . As I live," says the Lord GOD, "I have no pleasure in the death of the wicked, but that the wicked turn from his way and live. Turn, turn from your evil ways! For why should you die. . . ?"[26]

☪

"For if we go on sinning willfully after receiving the knowledge of the truth, there no longer remains a sacrifice for sins, but a certain terrifying expectation of judgment, and the fury of a fire which will consume the adversaries."[27]
The Writer of Hebrews

Notes

1   Isaiah 66:2.
2   Psalm 53:1.
3   Proverbs 18:2.
4   1 Corinthians 2:14, 1:18.
5   Proverbs 12:15.
6   Matthew 11:15.
7   All definitions are from *The American Heritage Dictionary* (Boston: Houghton Mifflin Co., 1985).
8   Hebrews 12:29, Nahum 2:10.
9   Proverbs 1:7, 9:10.
10   Genesis 3:14.
11   Exodus 7:17.
12   Isaiah 40:8.
13   Isaiah 55:11.
14   Deuteronomy 8:3.
15   Matthew 5:18.
16   John 10:35.
17   2 Timothy 3:16.
18   2 Peter 1:20-21.
19   Psalm 19:10.
20   John 6:68.
21   2 Timothy 3:16 (NIV).
22   John Piper, Sermon, Bethlehem Baptist Church, Minneapolis, MN.
23   Matthew 7:13.
24   John Piper, *Spectacular Sins* (Wheaton, IL: Crossway, 2008), 13.
25   Matthew 7:24-27.
26   Isaiah 65:1, Deuteronomy 30:19, Ezekiel 33:11 (NKJV).
27   Hebrews 10:26-27.

FEARING GOD

Appendix 1

*" . . .I know that it will be well for those who fear God, who
fear Him openly. "*[1]
Solomon, God's Servant

The fear of God is the most beautiful, powerful, meaningful, fulfilling, and, yes, exuberant place to live. If you call yourself a Christian and don't know that—you're doing it wrong.

You've not yet learned the indispensable lesson of this life—to tremble before your Creator with complete delight in abandoned worship. A deep peace and enduring joy arise through the sanctifying process of yielding to God as He crushes the hubris and self-importance out of our lives. This happens only as we learn God correctly, coming to fear Him as He has commanded. Truly, this is the most devastatingly humbling yet exquisitely enlightening epiphany a human being can experience.

For indeed, to genuinely fear the biblical God is to fear nothing else. To fear the biblical God is to be progressively liberated from every form of anxiety and temporal slavery. To fear the biblical God is to find the breathtaking purpose for which your soul and mind were created—namely, ever-intensifying, awed intimacy with your Maker.

The proper fear of God— this stunned wonder and captivated reverence—fully animates the human spirit and intellect. To walk in perpetual amazement of Yahweh is to be truly alive! To learn to consciously abide in the never-ending, ever-increasing wonderment of Jesus Christ is to fully live.

Denominations, creeds, confessions, and doctrinal orthodoxy alone can't touch this kind of profound, personal, life-altering experience. While some of the foregoing are useful, even needful, ultimately, they are merely a means to an end. God, the living, reigning, yes, fearsome Sovereign of heaven and earth is the true believer's end. We cannot settle for merely attending religious services and knowing biblical facts. We must encounter and know our Creator-Redeemer God in all His fullness. It is no matter that this pursuit starts in time and will ultimately consume a billion eternities—for it will be a billion eternities flawlessly spent!

Finding Fear—It's in the Seeking

Some readers profess to be Christians but there is no real fear of God in their hearts or minds. Here's how "belief" unfolded for some readers: As a rational person, you couldn't avoid the intellectual prerequisite that an eternal, omnipotent, personal Creator must be there—and yes, your parents took you to a Christian church—and yes, the God of the Bible provided the needed precondition for the created order, and so, there you have it—you "believe" in the Christian God. But honestly . . . God is really no more than a necessary, if not somewhat inconvenient, ideological presupposition. There has never been any real awe, reverence, fear, and trembling going on; not really. In fact, this fear-of-God talk is utterly alien to you and makes you more than a little uncomfortable.

This is obviously true for the nominal Christian and could, in part, be true for the newly born-again, immature Christian as well. The biblical prescription for both is the same. God tells us. "And you will seek Me and find Me, when you search for Me with all your heart. And I will be found by you, declares the LORD. . . ."[2] This is your solution. Whether you are an unlearned novice Christian, or merely a Christian in name only, you must seek God. And the Lord says, to genuinely seek Him is to always find Him. And to find God is to always find fear. Yeah, and to truly learn to fear the incensed and wrathful, yet longsuffering and merciful, Redeemer-God of the Bible is to finally remedy that nagging self-pity problem. For in rightly looking at the biblical God, we can no longer see ourselves as victims but as the rebels we've always been. Consequently, considering what we know we justly deserve from the hand of a holy God but as His adopted children will not receive, we will find it impossible to ever take anything for granted again—for indeed, EVERYTHING is grace!

Growing Fear—It's in the Looking

And how does the born-again person mature in the fear of God? It's simple. Look at Him. You must relentlessly look at God in His Word to grow the fear. The deeper you go in the Scriptures, the more "terrifyingly magnificent"[3] He will be in your mind's eye. This is why most professing Christians do not deeply fear God—they do not invest the time to thoughtfully look at Him in the Bible, meditating upon His manifold perfections.

Just a brief personal testimony here: I recently spent two years looking at God through the lens of Creation. It was two years, ear-deep in the science, in conjunction with the Word of God. I was just doing research. Just reading. Thinking. Inferring. Quantifying. Deliberating. Connecting dots. You know what happened, right? I was radically transformed in the process of immersing myself in the almighty, creative genius of the galaxy-breathing God! I am not the same. I fear Him more. I believe Him more. I trust Him more. I love Him more. I am now freer to obey Him beyond the comfort zone of cultural conformity. To yes, live outside the box of mere worldly convention. It all flowed out of that one long look at God and His omnipotent creative power, brilliance, and presence. Truly, He is infinitely beyond breathtaking!

And may I confess, the very same thing has happened to me in the writing of this book. Just looking at God in the Bible. Just reading His words. Just pouring over His historical record of judgment. Contemplating His promised end-times adjudications. Meditating on the reality and nature of an eternal hell. It's what the study of divine justice does in the regenerate heart—God gets higher, greater, holier. He is fearsome Other! If you persist in genuinely looking at Him in the Bible, you cannot not humbly worship!

Living Fear—It's in the Emancipation

How do you live out the fear of God? This may be the easiest part . . . *if* you have in fact genuinely found godly fear and are earnestly growing in that fear. For, in seeking God and looking at Him in His Word, we are being liberated! If you truly seek Him, you will find Him. It's His promise. And if you faithfully look at Him, you will be changed. The apostle is right, for in looking at God, we are, indeed, "being transformed."[4] In the seeking of God, and in the looking at God, we are, for the first time in our lives, learning real freedom. We are released, so to speak, from the "wisdom of the world,"[5] to joyfully flesh out the fear of God in genuinely following Him. It's just where the proper fear of the Lord takes you—absolute liberty. You simply can't live small anymore. Of course, Daniel was right: "The people that do know their God shall be strong, and do exploits."[6] Certainly, as noted, to fear God is to fear nothing else—that's ultimate emancipation from the carefully scripted lives of the largely anesthetized and mostly bored masses!

Practicing Fear—It's in the Obedience

If you're not proactively seeking God . . . if you're not proactively looking at God . . . if you're not proactively finding your freedom in God, you cannot, and will not, fear Him or follow Him as He has purposed. You must decide. Will you practice the fear of God? Meaning, will you live it out? Will you do it every day? Will you consciously seek God in His Word? Will you consciously look at God in His Word? Will you consciously embrace His freedom? Will you consciously obey God in accordance with His Word? Will you fight to bring the awe of God down into the minutiae of your everyday life? That's how you will know if you're doing it right or not. As noted in the Introduction, in practicing fear, awe will begin to seep into every corner of your life. You will learn to fear God in every sphere—for in abandoned obedience, we experience the breathtaking truth of John 14:21. Jesus says, "He who has My commandments and keeps them, he it is who loves Me; and he who loves Me, shall be loved by My Father, and I will love him, and will disclose Myself to him." This is the most exhilarating rush a human being can experience—divine disclosure. It perpetually amplifies in the obedience!

Moreover, in properly fearing God, we come to fully understand that it's not about us. And what a wonderful discovery that is! For we both know, neither one of us is that interesting. You really can't hold your own attention. Nor can I. Praise God, it's all about Him! The cosmos, and everyone in it, is for His glory. Yes, you, your soul, your life, your body, your sexuality, your singleness, your marriage, your kids, your career, your money, your hobbies, your plans, your dreams, your trials, your pain, your sicknesses, and finally your death are all meant to be for the glory of God. It's where the proper fear of God will take you. Everything in your life will be joyfully surrendered up to the One who gave you everything in your life. That's when you know without any doubt that you're doing it right!

Unpacking Fear—It's in the Delight

I know, many people don't like the sound of fearing God. Have you read Nehemiah? He writes, " . . .O LORD, let your ear be attentive to the prayer of your servant, and to the prayer of your servants who *delight* to fear your name..."[7] The Psalmist sings, "Worship the LORD with reverence, and *rejoice with trembling*."[8] The spiritual man, the wise man, "delights to fear" Yahweh and "rejoices with trembling." Ultimately, we were wired for this. The human soul was designed to experience heart-exploding awe, and the biblical God is the only One who can deliver. Fearing our Creator is life. It is purpose. It is meaning. It is fulfillment. It is joy. Regarding Jesus Christ, the prophet wrote, "And the Spirit of the LORD will rest on Him. . . . And He will *delight* in the fear of the LORD."[9] If the Son of God is to be our model, and of course He is, we must not fear the fear of the Lord, but aggressively pursue it and learn all the delights it affords!

Don't misunderstand. I am in no way seeking to explain away the fact that we are commanded and fitted to fear God. I am not seeking to mitigate the meaning of the word. Concerning God,

Isaiah was clear, " . . .He shall be your fear and He shall be your dread."[10] To borrow from Francis Chan, fear means fear, it needs no interpretation.[11] The dictionary gives this definition:

> **Fear** *n* 1. An emotion of alarm and agitation caused by the expectation or realization of danger. 2. Extreme reverence or awe, as toward a supreme power. 3. A ground for dread or apprehension; danger.[12]

Yes, He is a dangerous God! The proper fear of the Lord encompasses each of the above definitions, depending upon whether we are in relationship with Jesus Christ or not. As John Piper says, "There is terror when outside of Christ and a different kind of trembling when in Christ."[13] The rebel trembles one way; the disciple trembles in another! There is perfect fear and dread for the unbeliever. There is perfect fear and delight for the believer. I know no unbeliever can understand the distinction here, but I'm pretty sure no unbelievers are reading this book.

The Thrill of Fear—It's in the Knowing
Piper again:

> For most of us, fear is something we want to get rid of, not get more of. If that's true of the fear of the Lord, then there is something wrong with our hearts or something wrong with our understanding of this fear. Have you ever gathered up the spectacular promises made to those who fear God? They are so wonderful that you would think fearing God must be the most thrilling thing in the world—which it is.[14]

Here are God's promises to those who fear Him . . . Yes, thrilling is the proper adjective!

> **Psalm 25:14**—"The secret of the LORD is for those who fear Him, and He will make them know His covenant."
> **Psalm 33:18**—"Behold, the eye of the LORD is on those who fear Him. . . ."

Psalm 34:7—"The angel of the LORD encamps around those who fear Him, and rescues them."
Psalm 34:9—"O fear the LORD, you His saints; For to those who fear Him, there is no want."
Psalm 103:13—". . .The LORD has compassion on those who fear Him."
Psalm 103:17—"But the lovingkindness of the LORD is from everlasting to everlasting on those who fear Him. . . ."
Psalm 147:11—"The LORD favors those who fear Him. . . ."
Proverbs 19:23—"The fear of the LORD leads to life. . . ."

Dangerous God says for those who fear Me there is My secret, My watch-care, My rescue, My provision, My compassion, My everlasting lovingkindness, My favor, and My forever life! And yes! Yes, as the psalmist sings, "There is forgiveness with You, that You may be feared."[15]

In genuinely coming to fear the Lord, we will never face His wrath, vengeance, recompense, and terror. We will not meet God as an enemy. We will come before Him as "fellow heirs with Christ."[16]

To the thinking person, I simply ask—what more could there possibly be to say?

✍

". . .work out you own salvation with fear and trembling; for it is God who is at work in you, both to will and to work for His good pleasure."[17]
Paul, God's Apostle

NOTES

1   Ecclesiastes 8:12.
2   Jeremiah 29:13-14.
3   John Piper, *Spectacular Sins* (Wheaton, IL: Crossway, 2008), 13.
4   2 Corinthians 3:18.
5   1 Corinthians 1:20.
6   Daniel 11:32 (KJV).
7   Nehemiah 1:11 (ESV).
8   Psalm 2:11.
9   Isaiah 11:2-3.
10   Isaiah 8:13.
11   Francis Chan, "I'm Leaving in 2020 Be Fishers of Men" November 6, 2019, accessed December 12, 2019, https://www.youtube.com/watch?v=bnxdk9SZUqw.
12   From *The American Heritage Dictionary* (Boston: Houghton Mifflin Co., 1985).
13   John Piper, Ask Pastor John, "What Does It Mean for the Christian to Fear God?" April 1, 2014, accessed December 8, 2019, https://www.desiringgod.org/interviews/what-does-it-mean-for-the-christian-to-fear-god.
14   John Piper, *A Godward Life* (Sisters, OR: Multnomah Publishers, 1997), 246.
15   Psalm 130:4.
16   Romans 8:17.
17   Philippians 2:12-13.

A FAIR QUESTION AND
A PLAUSIBLE INFERENCE

Appendix 2

"A truthful witness saves lives, but he who utters lies is treacherous."[1]

Solomon, God's Servant

God's Wrath—The Balance Question

Some have asked a very good question concerning the book. Where is the balance? While the Cross (Chapter Nine) is ballast enough, I wonder, why do we always seem to feel the need to moderate or soften God's wrath anytime we speak of it? "Dying the death of a thousand qualifications"[2] is what American theologian Michael Horton writes regarding a proper and scripturally informed fear of God. I am quite sure I've never heard God's love mitigated in this way. Yes, we're all aware of God's love. If we've been to a church once in our lives, we know this about God— His love is the principal subject of 90 percent of the sermons preached everywhere in the world every Sunday morning. This book is a meager attempt to begin to balance the scales. Indeed, it would take a thousand such books and tens of thousands of sermons to even partially launch the urgently needed return to a more biblically honest view of God.

So please understand, the goal of this book is not one of balance. It is a simple attempt to provide a thoroughly biblical exposé of God's righteous judgment of mankind—an adjudication provoked by our arrogant and presumptuous rebellion. And no, in this book I haven't reminded you that God's anger is altogether unlike that of an irate, out-of-control human being . . . I haven't explicitly told you that God's ire is a controlled, principled, measured, disciplined indignation . . . I haven't stated that God is not a sadistic God, bent upon inflicting as much harm as He possibly can. I haven't told you these things because you, my target audience, are biblically literate. I need not bore you with the blatantly obvious.

God's Wrath—The Unbalanced Inference

Nothing makes sense if God doesn't make sense. Read what this secular intellectual had to say about the one-dimensional god of love she has always heard about.

> I don't find the idea of a personal, loving God consistent with what I see in the daily massacre of the innocent. To me it's a hard claim to make when [God] is willing to allow horrific things to happen . . . I cannot stomach what appears to be a patently false claim about a personal, loving God. . . .

Her notion of the Christian God is due largely to how your average preacher preaches, how your average Christian author writes, and how your average Christian talks about God. Consequently, she has a wholly unbalanced view of her Creator. If the biblical God is only love, with no other emotional characteristics and attributes, then one could argue she has drawn a plausible inference. But, the God of Scripture is not one-dimensional. A half-truth is always a lie. Solomon is right, as noted above: half-truths are "treacherous."

Do you see the damage done in presenting an enfeebled and redacted god as many so-called ministers and Christians do today? This one-sided view of her Creator that she has always heard about distorts her view of everything else. She backhandedly infers that if there is a God, He could not be loving. Yes, an erroneous conclusion, but one that is fostered by the churches' virtually

universal practice of preaching an edited god. By not prominent-
ly proclaiming man's unqualified accountability in subjecting
the world to evil and God's righteous judgment thereon, myriad
false conclusions are unendingly drawn. To omit man's premeditated mutiny against his Creator and God's resultant holy wrath
is to present a truncated biblical message—one that brings many
to the same erroneous deduction of this scholar.

Why do we, in her words, observe "the daily massacre of the
innocent?" Why do we witness "horrific things"? Because in de-
ciding against God, we willfully chose evil, rightfully incurring
God's awful wrath. This intellectual's unbalanced view of God
drives her to an unbalanced view of man, resulting in an unbalanced interpretation of the world around her. A biblical worldview understands that humanity is not innocent, and that nothing in all the cosmos is more horrific than mankind's insurgence
against his good, benevolent, and holy Creator. Without a biblically balanced view of God, nothing makes sense and, in due
course, God is inevitably doubted and ultimately slandered.

♫

"The knowledge of the Holy One is understanding."[3]
Solomon, God's Servant

NOTES

1   Proverbs 14:25.

2   Michael Horton, "What Are You Afraid Of," White Horse Inn Blog, March 19, 2020, accessed March 22, 2020, https://www.whitehorseinn.org/2020/03/what-are-you-afraid-of/.

3   Proverbs 9:10.

THE JUSTICE OF GOD IN THE DAMNATION OF SINNERS

Appendix 3

". . .that every mouth may be stopped, and all the world may
become guilty before God."[1]
Paul, God's Apostle

Following are excerpts from eighteenth-century American theologian, Jonathan Edwards' widely commended sermon entitled, *The Justice of God in the Damnation of Sinners*[2] which he pointedly directed at the impenitent, including nominal Christians.

"[God] is originally under no obligation to keep men from sinning; but may in His providence permit and leave them to sin. . . . It is unreasonable to suppose, that God should be obliged, if He makes a reasonable creature capable of knowing His will, and receiving a law from Him, and being subject to His moral government, at the same time to make it impossible for [angels or men] to sin or break His law. . . ."

". . .God by His sovereignty has a right to determine about [man's] redemption as He pleases. He has a right to determine whether He will redeem any or not. He might, if He had pleased, have left all to perish. . . ."

"It is [proper] that God should order all . . . things according to His pleasure. By reason of His greatness and glory . . . He is worthy that He should make Himself His end . . . without asking leave or counsel of any, and without giving account of any of His matters."

". . .It would be just and righteous with God eternally to reject and destroy you. This is what you are in danger of. . . . You who are a Christ-less sinner . . . you have reason to tremble every moment. But be you [ever] so much afraid of it [and] eternal damnation be ever so dreadful, yet it is just . . . God's justice may be glorious in it. The dreadfulness of the thing on your part, and the greatness of your dread of it, do not render it the less righteous on God's part."

"If God should forever cast you off, it would be exactly agreeable to your treatment of Him . . . you, who never have exercised the least degree of love to God in all your life. . . . You have no benevolence in your heart toward God; you never rejoiced in God's happiness. . . . Why then should God be looked upon as obliged to take so much care for your happiness?"

"You care not what becomes of God's glory; you are not distressed how much His honor seems to suffer in the world: why should God care anymore for your welfare? Has it not been so, that if you could but promote your private interest, and gratify your own lusts, you cared not how much the glory of God suffered? And why may not God advance His own glory in the ruin of your welfare, not caring how much your interest suffers by it? You never so much as stirred one step, sincerely making the glory of God your end, or acting from real respect to Him. . . . You were not willing to deny yourself for God; you never cared to put yourself out of your way for Christ; whenever anything . . . difficult came in your way, that the glory of God was concerned in, it has been your manner to shun it, and excuse yourself from it. You did not care to hurt yourself for Christ, whom you did not see worthy of it; and why then must it be looked upon as a hard and cruel thing, if Christ is not pleased to spill His blood and be tormented to death for such a sinner?"

"You have slighted God; and why then may not God justly slight you. . . . You have slighted the honor of God and valued it no more than the dirt under your feet. You have been told that such things were contrary to the will of a holy God, and against His honor; but you cared not for that. God called upon you, and exhorted you to be more tender of His honor; but you went on without regarding Him. . . . And yet is it hard that God should slight you? Are you more honorable than God, that He must be obliged to make much of you, how light however you make of Him and His glory?"

"You indeed make a pretense and show of honoring Him in your prayers, and attendance on other external duties. . . . You weep for yourself; you are afraid of hell; and do you think that is worthy of God to take much notice of you, because you can cry when you are in danger of being damned; when at the same time you indeed care nothing for God's honor. Seeing you thus disregard so great a God, is it a heinous thing for God to slight you. . . ?"

"Why should God be looked upon as obliged to bestow salvation upon you, when you have been so ungrateful for the mercies, He has bestowed upon you already? God has [shown] you a great deal of kindness, and He never has sincerely been thanked by you for any of it. God has watched over you, and preserved you, and provided for you, and followed you with mercy all your days; and yet you have continued sinning against Him. He has given you food and clothing. . . . He has preserved you while you slept. . . . God, notwithstanding your ingratitude, has still continued His mercy; but His kindness has never won your heart. . . . But what thanks has God received for it? What kind of returns have you made for all this kindness? As God has multiplied mercies, so you have multiplied provocations."

"You have voluntarily chosen to be with Satan in his enmity and opposition to God; how justly therefore might you be with him in his punishment! You did not choose to be on God's side, but rather chose to side with the devil, and have obstinately continued in it, against God's often repeated calls and counsels. . . . You have given yourself up to [Satan] . . . how justly therefore may God also give you up to him, and leave you in his power, to accomplish your ruin! Seeing as you have yielded yourself to [Satan's] will, to do as he would have you, surely God may leave you in his hands to execute his will upon you. If men will be with God's enemy, and on his side, why is God obliged to redeem them out of his hands. . . . Doubtless you would be glad to serve the devil, and be God's enemy while you live, and then to have God your friend, and deliver you from the devil, when you come to die. But will God be unjust if He deals otherwise with you? No, surely! It will be altogether and perfectly just, that you should have your portion with him with whom you have chosen to work . . . and if you cry to God for deliverance, He may most justly give you [the answer of] Judges 10:14, "Go to the gods which you have chosen."

"Consider how often you have refused to hear God's calls to you, and how just it would therefore be, if He should refuse to hear you when you call to Him. You are ready . . . to complain that you have often prayed and earnestly begged of God to show you mercy, and yet have no answer. . . . But do you consider how often God has called, and you have denied Him? Was it no crime for you to refuse to hear when God called? And yet is it now very hard that God does not hear your earnest calls, and that though your calling on God be not from any respect to Him, but merely from self-love?"

"Have you not taken encouragement to sin against God, on that very presumption, that God would show you mercy when you sought it? And may not God justly refuse you that mercy that you have so presumed upon? . . .how righteous therefore would it be in God, to disappoint such a wicked presumption! It was upon that very hope that you dared to affront the majesty of heaven so dreadfully as you have done; and can you now be so [foolish] as to think that God is obliged not to frustrate that hope? . . .must God be accounted hard because He will not do according to such a sinners' presumption? . . . Cannot He be excused from showing such a sinner mercy when he is pleased to seek it, without incurring the charge of being unjust. Consider, that you have . . . been the worst enemy to Him, for His being a merciful God. So, have you treated the attribute of God's mercy! How just is it therefore that you never should have any benefit of that attribute!"

"There is such base and horrid ingratitude, in being the worse to God because He is a being of infinite goodness and grace. . . . The greater the mercy of God is, the more should you be engaged to love Him, and to live to His glory. But it has been contrariwise with you; the consideration of the mercies of God being so exceeding great, is the thing [in which] you have encouraged yourself in sin. You have heard that the mercy of God was without bounds, that it was sufficient to pardon the greatest sinner, and you have upon that very account ventured to be a very great sinner . . . you heard that He was a very merciful God, and had grace enough to pardon you, and so cared not how offensive your sins were to Him. . . . Now, how righteous would it be if God should swear in His wrath, that you should never be the better for His being infinitely merciful!"

"You have taken encouragement to sin the more, for [the] consideration that Christ came in the world and died to save sinners; such thanks has Christ had from you. . . . Now, how justly might God refuse that you should ever be the better for His Son's laying down His life! It was because of these things that you put off seeking salvation. You would take the pleasures of sin still longer, hardening yourself because mercy was infinite, and it would not be too late, if you sought it afterwards; now, how justly may God disappoint you in this, and so order it that it shall be too late!"

"How have some of you risen up against God, and in the frame of your minds opposed Him in His sovereign dispensations! And how justly upon that account might God oppose you and set Himself against you! You . . . have dared to find fault and quarrel with God. . . . You have taken upon [yourself] to call God to an account, why He does thus and thus. . . . If you have been restrained by fear from openly venting your opposition and enmity of heart against God's government, yet it has been in you . . . tolerating blasphemous thoughts and malignant risings of heart against Him. . . . Now, seeing you have thus opposed God, how just is it that God should oppose you! Or is it because you are so much better, and so much greater than God, that it is a crime for Him to make that opposition against you which you make against Him? Do you think . . . that you may be an enemy to God, but God must by no means be an enemy to you. . . ?"

". . .if you should be eternally cast off by God, it would be most agreeable to your behavior towards Him; which appears by this, that you reject Christ and will not have Him for your Savior. If God offers you a Savior from deserved punishment, and you will not receive Him, then surely it is just that you should go without a Savior. Or is God obliged, because you do not like this Savior, to provide you another? . . .now if you refuse to accept [Christ], is God therefore unjust if He does not save you? Is He obliged to save you in a way of your own choosing, because you do not like the way of His choosing?"

"There is a great deal of difference between a willingness not to be damned, and . . . being willing to receive Christ for your Savior . . . persons very commonly mistake the one for the other, they are quite two [different] things. You may love the deliverance but hate the deliverer. . . . The inclination of your will goes no further than self, it never reaches Christ. You are willing not to be miserable; that is, you love yourself, and there your will and choice terminate. . . . There is certainly a great deal of difference between a forced compliance and a free-will willingness. . . . Now that willingness, whereby you think you are willing to have Christ for a Savior, is merely a forced thing. Your heart does not go out after Christ of itself, but you are forced and driven to seek an interest in Him. Christ has no share at all in your heart. This forced compliance is not what Christ seeks of you; He seeks a free and willing acceptance. . . . And if you refuse thus to receive Christ, how just is that Christ should refuse to receive you? Who can rationally expect that Christ should force Himself upon any man to be His Savior?"

"But how can you be willing to have Christ for a Savior from [the recompense] of hell, if you be not sensible that you [are deserving] of hell? If you have not really deserved everlasting burnings in hell, then the very offer of an atonement for such is an imposition upon you. . . . A man who is not convinced that he has deserved so dreadful a punishment, cannot willingly submit to be charged with it. If he thinks he is willing, it is but a mere forced feigned business; because in his heart he looks upon himself greatly injured; and therefore he cannot freely accept Christ. . . . Such a one cannot like the way of salvation by Christ; for he thinks he has not deserved hell, then he will think that freedom from hell is a debt; and therefore cannot willingly and heartily receive it as a free gift—he [has] judged himself unjustly condemned."

"In the way of salvation by Christ, men's own goodness is wholly set at naught . . . [and] you [are not] willing to be saved in a way wherein your own goodness is set at naught, as is evident, since you make much of it yourself. You make much of your prayers and pains in religion and are often thinking of them; how considerable do they appear to you, when you look back upon them! And some of you are thinking how much more you have done than others and expecting some respect or regard that God should manifest to what you do. Now, if you make so much of what you do yourself, it is impossible that you should be freely willing that God should make nothing of it."

"Seeing therefore it is so evident, that you refuse to accept . . . Christ as your Savior, why is Christ to be blamed that He does not save you? Christ has offered Himself to you, to be your Savior in time past, and He continues offering Himself still, and you continue to reject Him, and yet complain that He does not save you—So strangely unreasonable, and inconsistent with themselves, are gospel sinners! . . . Sinners therefore spend their time in foolish arguing and objecting, making much of that which is good for nothing, making those excuses that are not worth offering. It is vain to keep making objection. You stand justly condemned. The blame lies at your door."

"The heinousness of this sin of rejecting a Savior especially appears in two things: (1) The greatness of the benefits offered. (2) The wonderfulness of the way in which these benefits are procured and offered. . . . Surely you might justly be cast into hell without one more offer of a Savior! Yea, and thrust down in the lowest hell! Herein you have exceeded the devils; for they never rejected the offers of such glorious mercy; no, nor any mercy at all. This will be the distinguishing condemnation of gospel-sinners. . . ."

"If God should forever cast you off and destroy you, it would be agreeable to your treatment of others. It would be no other than what would be exactly answerable to your behavior towards your fellow creatures. . . ."

"If God should eternally cast you off, it would but be agreeable to your own behaviors towards yourself . . . in being so careless of your own salvation. You have refused to take care for your salvation, as God has counseled and commanded you from time to time; and why may not God neglect it, now [that] you seek it of Him? Is God obliged to be more careful of your happiness, then you are either of your own happiness or His glory? Is God bound to take that care for you, out of love to you, that you will not take for yourself, either from love to yourself, or regard to His authority?"

"How long, and how greatly, have you neglected the welfare of your precious soul, refusing to take pains and deny yourself, or put yourself a little out of your way for your salvation, while God has been calling upon you! Neither your duty to God, nor love to your own soul, were enough to induce you to do little things for your own welfare; and yet do you now expect that God should do great things, putting forth almighty power, and exercising infinite mercy for it . . . Now how justly might God order it so, that it should be too late, leaving you to seek in vain. . . . How justly therefore may God leave you to be undone!"

"You have destroyed yourself . . . willfully, contrary to God's repeated counsels, yea, and destroyed yourself in fighting against

God. Now therefore, why do you blame any but yourself if you are destroyed? . . .You would have your own way, and did not like that God should oppose you in it, and your way was to ruin your own soul; how just therefore is it, if now at length, God ceases to oppose you, and falls in with you, and lets your soul be ruined; and as you would destroy yourself, so should put to His hand to destroy you too! . . .If you would run into the fire against all restraints both of God's mercy and authority, you must even blame yourself if you are burnt."

"Thus I have proposed some things to your consideration, which, if you are not exceeding[ly] blind, senseless, and perverse, will stop your mouth, and convince you that you stand justly condemned before God; and that He would in no wise deal hardly with you, but altogether justly, in denying you any mercy, and He may cast you into eternal destruction, without any regard to your welfare, denying you converting grace, and giving you over to Satan, and at last cast you into the lake that burns with fire and brimstone, to be there to eternity, having no rest day or night, forever glorifying His justice upon you in the presence of the holy angels, and in the presence of the Lamb."

"The thing at bottom is, that men have low thoughts of God, and high thoughts of themselves; and therefore it is that they look upon God as having so little right, and they so much. . . . God may justly show greater respect to others than to you, for you have shown greater respect to others than to God. You have rather chosen to offend God than men. . . . You have shown a greater regard to wicked men than to God; you have honored them more, loved them better, and adhered to them rather than to Him. Yea, you have honored the devil, in many respects, more than God: you have chosen his will and his interest, rather than God's will and His glory: you have chosen a little [dishonorable gain], rather than God: you have set more by a vile lust than by Him: you have chosen these things, and rejected God. You have set your heart on these things, and cast God behind your back. . . . You have shown greater respect to vile and worthless things, and no respect to God's glory; and why may not God set

His love on others, and have no respect to your happiness? You have shown great respect to others, and not to God, whom you are laid under infinite obligations to respect above all; and why may not God show respect to others, and not to you. . . ?"

"I will finish what I have to say to [lost] men in the application of this doctrine, with a caution not to improve the doctrine to discouragement. For though it would be righteous in God [to] forever cast you off, and destroy you, yet it would also be just in God to save you, in and through Christ, who has made complete satisfaction for all sin. . . . Yea, God may, through this Mediator, not only justly, but honorably, show you mercy. The blood of Christ is so precious, that it is fully sufficient to pay the debt you have contracted, and perfectly to vindicate the Divine Majesty from all the dishonor cast upon it, by these many great sins of yours. . . . So that you need not be at all discouraged from seeking mercy, for there is enough in Christ."

"I would conclude this discourse by putting the godly in mind of the freeness and wonderfulness of the grace of God towards them. For such were the same of you—the case was just so with you as you have heard; you had such a wicked heart, you lived such a wicked life, and it would have been most just with God forever to have cast you off: but He has had mercy upon you; He has made his glorious grace appear in your everlasting salvation. You had no love to God; but yet He has exercised unspeakable love to you. You have [treated God with contempt] . . .but so great a value has God's grace set on you and your happiness, that you have been redeemed at the price of the blood of His own Son. You chose to be with Satan in his service; but yet God has made you a joint heir with Christ of his glory. You were ungrateful for past mercies; yet God not only continued those mercies but bestowed unspeakably greater mercies upon you. You refused to hear when God called; yet God heard you when you called. You abused the infiniteness of God's mercy to encourage yourself in sin against Him; yet God has manifested the infiniteness of that mercy, in the exercises of it towards you. . . . You have neglected your own salvation; but God has not neglected it. You have destroyed yourself; but yet in God has been your help. God has magnified His free grace towards you, and not to others; because He has chosen you, and it hath pleased Him to set His love upon you."

"O what cause is here for praise! What obligations you are under to bless the Lord who has dealt bountifully with you and magnify His holy name! What cause for you to praise God in humility, to walk humbly before him. . . . You shall never open your mouth in boasting, or self-justification; but lie the lower before God for His mercy to you. You have reason, the more abundantly, to open your mouth in God's praises, that they may be continually in your mouth, both here and to all eternity, for His rich, unspeakable, and sovereign mercy to you, whereby He, and He alone, has made you to differ from others."

NOTES

1   Romans 3:19 (NKJV).
2   Jonathan Edwards, "The Justice of God in the Damnation of Sinners," accessed May 11, 2018, http://www.biblebb.com/files/edwards/je-justice.htm - [Minor additions for clarity only].

ABOUT THE AUTHOR

At the age of forty-two, Jim left a twenty-year business career to answer God's call to preach. Since early 2004, he and his wife, Karen, have lived in Milan, Italy, where Jim is the pastor of the International Church of Milan, a non-denominational, Bible-believing, and Bible-teaching church ministering to internationals from every corner of the globe. He is also author of *Uncareful Lives: Walking Where Feet May Fail* (Ambassador Publications) and *Everything Says, "Glory!": Science Exposes Darwinian Folklore* (Great Writing Publications).

Learn more about Jim Albright at
http://www.greatwriting.org/author-albright

You can find Jim's sermons at
https://pastorjimpodcast.podbean.com/

www.dangerousgod.com

God is probably not who you think He is...

... Sure, you have some concept of a supreme being—but, is your god-notion, God? The one true God? The biblical God? The God who is?

To anyone who has ears to hear, I simply say that it's time to open the Book and truly behold the dreadful holiness and terrifying awe of I AM. Certainly, it is long past time in this era of low-resolution preaching, denominational banality, and pervasive biblical illiteracy. For indeed, the Bible is unmistakably clear...

"It is a terrifying thing to fall into the hands of the living God."
(Hebrews 10:31)

"Euphemistic thinking about God is not truthful thinking about God. . . . This book, as shocking as it might be, is a needed corrective."—*Pastor Jim Elliff*

". . . a call to a serious reconsideration of our weak, contemporary ideas of God. . ."—*Professor Jim Ehrhard*

". . . *Dangerous God* . . . deflated my pride, exposed my man-centeredness, and rekindled my fear of the Lord to the praise of His glory and the joy of my soul."—*Pastor Brad Vaden*

"*Dangerous God* is not like any other book you will likely find in the twenty-first century. Albright dares to declare the true nature of the God who inhabits the universe."—*Pastor Keith Jones*

". . . a no-holds-barred exposé of the God no one wants to talk about. . . . You owe it to yourself, your loved ones, and your neighbors to read it."—*Pastor Alan Johnston*

Jim Albright: At the age of forty-two, Jim left a twenty-year business career to answer God's call to preach. Since early 2004, he and his wife, Karen, have lived in Milan, Italy, where Jim is the pastor of the International Church of Milan, a non-denominational, Bible-believing, and Bible-teaching church ministering to internationals from around the globe.

GREAT WRITING
PUBLICATIONS

www.greatwriting.org

978-1-7343452-7-8

9 781734 345278

BISAC CLASSIFICATION: REL067000
RELIGION / Christian Theology / General